Identity
An International Journal of Theory and Research

First published 2002 by Lawrence Erlbaum Associates, Inc.

Published 2019 by Routledge
2 Park Square, Milton Park, Abingdon, Oxon OX14 4RN
52 Vanderbilt Avenue, New York, NY 10017

Routledge is an imprint of the Taylor & Francis Group, an informa business

Copyright © 2002 Taylor & Francis

All rights reserved. No part of this book may be reprinted or reproduced or utilised in any form or by any electronic, mechanical, or other means, now known or hereafter invented, including photocopying and recording, or in any information storage or retrieval system, without permission in writing from the publishers.

Notice:
Product or corporate names may be trademarks or registered trademarks, and are used only for identification and explanation without intent to infringe.

ISBN 13: 978-0-8058-9674-9 (pbk)
ISSN 1528–3488.

Identity
An International Journal of Theory and Research
Volume 2, Number 2

Special Issue: Diasporic Identity: Myth, Culture, and the Politics of Home

Guest Editor:
Anton Allahar
University of Western Ontario

National Identity, Instrumental Identifications and the Caribbean's   115
Culture of "Play"
  Anthony Maingot

Racial Politics and Cultural Identity in Trinidad's Carnival   125
  Amanda Lynn Zavitz and Anton L. Allahar

Pariah Status, Identity, and Creativity in Babylon: 147
Utopian Visions of "Home" in the African Diaspora
  Janet L. DeCosmo

Colón Man Version: Oppositional Narratives and Jamaican   157
Identity in Michael Thelwell's *The Harder They Come*
  Rhonda D. Frederick

The Geopolitics of Identity: Popular Literature, Censorship,   177
and the Spanish Media
  Mireya Folch-Serra

Book Review Section

New Perspectives on Racial Identity Development: 193
A Theoretical and Practical Anthology
Edited by Charmaine L. Wijeyesinghe and Bailey W. Jackson III
  Jean Phinney

Society for Research on Identity Formation

President
Alan Waterman..The College of New Jersey

President Elect
James Côté..University of Western Ontario

Past President
Philip Dreyer..Claremont Graduate School

Treasurer
William Kurtines...Florida International University

Secretary
Marilyn Montgomery....................................Florida International University

Members-at-Large
Janet Gebelt..University of Portland
Joseph White..South Dakota State University

Student Members-at-Large
Nora Dunbar...University of Minnesota
Tommy Phillips..Auburn University

Membership information is available at SRIF@FIU.EDU

National Identity, Instrumental Identifications, and the Caribbean's Culture of "Play"

Anthony P. Maingot
Department of Sociology
Florida International University

The ability of West Indians to have multiple identifications, "to play the field" yet sustain a strong personal, participatory national identity shows that in their own way they have achieved freedom of the human condition. And, not trivially, this freedom is a double-edged sword. On the positive side, it reverts to their personal benefits and through that to real benefits to their islands. Evidence of such benefits are the steady flow of remittances and the money-spending tourism to the "home" country. On the negative side is the continued insularity and parochialism that prevents broader alliances of an enduring political type. Although good at coalescing for specific tactical and strategic ends, each island remains a "nation." The hope for a "West Indian nation" is as remote as it ever was.

In sociology, the idea of purposeful, instrumental play in social interaction has a distinguished pedigree. Classical thinkers such as Georg Simmel, Charles Horton Cooley, and George Herbert Mead and more contemporary ones such as Herbert Blumer and Erving Goffman established the bona fides of what is today called symbolic interactionism (Coser, 1977). Goffman (1959) in particular was interested in the dramaturgical aspects in the presentation of self. His concept of "impression management" described the way the individual attempted to manipulate the impressions and opinions others formed of him or her. This impression management included the use of "expressive equipment" and status symbols such as dress, but also, quite important, the use of speech patterns, facial expressions, and body gestures. Goffman's analysis is of relevance to the study of social interaction generally, but perhaps even more so in cultures where speech and gesture are of

---

Requests for reprints should be sent to Anthony P. Maingot, Department of Sociology, Florida International University, Miami, FL 33199. E-mail: maingota@fiu.edu

particular importance in impression management. One such culture is found in the English-speaking Caribbean (here referred to as the West Indies). The following anecdote illustrates the general outlines of how, and how frequently, impression management works in these territories.

Somewhere between the Guyanese towns of Georgetown and New Amsterdam, the taxi driver looked in the rearview mirror and asked, "What do you do?" "I'm Trinidadian, and I am a university professor," I responded, slipping back—as I tend to do when back home—into a Trinidadian accent. (For a review of the literature stressing shifting patterns of attitudes or adjustment in the acculturation process, see Berry, 1980, pp. 211–279). He seemed to ponder my answer (and probably my accent) for a minute, and then with an audible change of tone in his voice, inquired: "At what level do you want me to pitch my conversation?"

I was amused but neither surprised nor perplexed. I knew that I was sharing the enclosed space of the car with what Abrahams (1983) called the West Indian "man-of-words." Given who his passenger was, this Guyanese man-of-words had decided to enter into what Abrahams called the "fancy talker" mode. The "performance" had been engaged on both sides. Abrahams had elucidated such situations: "The man-of-words," he noted, "exhibits his talents best in contest with the performers" (p. xvi). One would have thought it an asymmetrical contest, given the evident differences of skin color, education, and, therefore, social class. Nothing of the sort. "Performances," said Abrahams, "must be judged on their ability to contend with opposing and competing forces" (p. xvi), and to keep the contest going indefinitely. Absolutely critical to making this possible are a capacity for "social maneuverability and psychological resilience," both capacities my taxi driver demonstrated to have in abundance.

Abrahams (1983) has not been alone in emphasizing the West Indian's capacity for "play," for adapting to different circumstances. Indeed, Burton (1997) traced the works of such outstanding anthropologists of the Caribbean as Manning, Lieber, Yelvington, and Brana-Shute to Wilson's 1973 book, *Crab Antics*. Based in the diminutive Colombian yet English-speaking island of Providencia, Wilson's book described a world of "play," a range of linguistic-rhetorical postures—that he (Wilson) considered distinct but complementary value systems. The same individual's behavior could oscillate between the respectable (i.e., proper to the salon or formal meeting, and characterized by what Abrahams called fancy or "sweet" talk) to behavior proper to the street corner or rum shop. Abrahams called the talk of the latter behavior "reputation" because it sought to establish one's equality through verbal self-affirmation with the male group.

The point is that none of these studies portrays these often stark shifts in behavior and presentation of self as anything other than convenient (i.e., strategic adjustments to different circumstances). This capacity for social maneuverability involves choices. These choices are not, however, random or purely voluntaristic. Each response is finely calibrated to meet the social exigencies of any given social structure and stratification system.

The fact that my taxi driver "played" to be my equal, and I his, did not eliminate the social-structural reality and the statuses we occupied within it. What his switch into fancy talk did, however, was demonstrate his capacity to contest and confront my higher social status. Even though it was evident he was using the cultural traits and verbal skills of his passenger, who was of higher status or class, his behavior was the exact opposite of deference: It was the resistance to deference. As Burton noted, West Indians draw on the materials furnished by the dominant culture (language in particular) to modify the relationship and "to turn against the dominant culture in order to contest that culture" (Burton, as quoted in Abrahams, 1983, p. 7). Ironically, this challenge or opposition also has the unintended consequence of reinforcing the status quo. It is not, therefore, rebellion in the collective sense, but rather rebellious self-assertion.

Despite that singularly North American propensity to assume otherwise, it should be evident that this psychological resilience has nothing to do with self-hatred or with trying to play White. West Indians do not shift language and behavior only in front of Whites. It is a generalized style of behavior that is assumed to accommodate whatever context they happen to be in and thereby maximize the possible gains from that accommodation, whether it be the formal banquet, the rum shop, or indeed, the taxi.

It is this capacity for strategic shifts in attitudes and allegiances that has so often come in for harsh criticism. A particularly noteworthy case, because it is so widely read, is the acerbic pen of Naipaul, himself a migrant from Trinidad. In his 1972 collection of short stories, *The Overcrowded Barracoon,* he portrayed the West Indian as a "mimic," always wishing to be someone else or somewhere else. What he repeatedly called "Carnival lunacy" has to do with people who "have seen themselves as futile, on the other side of the real world" (p. 247). They are, he said, "cut off from this [larger] world by reasons of geography, history, race" (p. 253).

To Naipaul (1967), the islanders are "a melodramatic race" [who] do not let pass occasions for public display, [people with] no complicating loyalties or depths" (p. 66). To him, such "psychological versatility and adaptability is supineness." West Indian politicians in particular, he said, "mistake words and the acclamation of words for power." As soon as their bluff is called, they are "lost."

And yet, Naipaul (1967) himself—in his own life and according to his own telling—has not been able to escape this pervasive West Indian capacity to, in his own words, "play the game." Note this piece of autobiography:

In London I had no guide ... no one to note my consistencies or inconsistencies. It was up to me to choose my character, and I chose the character that was easiest and most attractive [to me]. (p. 5)

One critical test of the hypothesis that West Indians gain advantages from their adaptability and maneuverability—from being able to play the game—is to undertake a brief review of the West Indian success in quickly adapting to quite different societies and cultures. A clear example of this is the West Indian as immigrant.

PLAY AND SUCCESSFUL ADAPTATION

In his autobiographical novel, *In the Castle of My Skin*, Lamming (1953) provided the classical account of a West Indian as a migrant. However, the novel covers only the initial stages of the move: The protagonist's sense of comfort with his Barbadian identity and the natural apprehensions as to what his new home will hold for him.

In a touching introduction to the book, the American novelist Richard Wright addressed the question of migration. To Wright, Lamming's autobiographical account of his migration indicated a story that was "above all, a record of shifting, troubled feelings groping their way toward a future that frightens as much as it beckons" (Wright as cited in Lamming, 1953, p. ix). Wright described the protagonist's intention of migrating as a horrifying prospect:

> The act of ripping the sensitive human personality from one's culture and the planting of that personality in another culture is a tortured, convoluted process. (p. ix)

Clearly unacquainted with Barbadian and West Indian history and culture, Wright (as cited in Lamming, 1953) saw Lamming ("Trumper" in the novel) as he saw his Black compatriots in the United States: "Frantically seeking a new identity." It is a telling point that Wright's position was in tune with much of the social science literature on migration and settlement. It had become customary in the study of migration to make a sharp distinction between internal and international migration. The assumption was that the difference was both qualitative and quantitative, that in both cases, fundamentally, it related to the type and degree of stress the migrant went through. Immigration was portrayed as causing considerably more serious psychological states than internal migration. As Sanua (1980) noted: "In general, such variables as immigration, mobility, acculturation and detribalization have been found to be related to psychiatric problems" (p. 226). This has been in much of the literature in psychology and sociology. The general assumption was that all migrants experience a steady cycle of adaptations that involves stressful "assimilation," difficult "accommodation," followed by "submission," "contention," and finally "revitalization" (Kurokawa, 1970).

This notion of stress in the migratory process is still alive and well in the literature. "Leaving one's native land for another country known only by reputation," says a popular textbook in race and ethnic relations, "can be an awe-inspiring experience" (Parrillo, 2000, p. 136). The concept of "culture shock" describes the contact with an unfamiliar cultural milieu that "jolts one's world of reality" and produces crises of "identity" (Parrillo, 2000, p. 136).

Patterson (1978) pursued this line of theoretical interpretation even farther. In Caribbean societies, he argued, migration "dominates and defines the social structure," and this has created a "modal personality syndrome devoid of trust and seemingly incapable of compromise" (p. 120). Both at home and abroad, the West Indian is portrayed as unbending and psychologically intractable. As such, said Patterson, migration is an obstacle to good government, with the elite willing and able to "use migration as a weapon against any progressive policy" (p. 120) to correct the conditions that make migration both possible and necessary.

The problem with such an approach to migration (call it the "psychopathology school"), is that it is belied by the whole, and long, history of West Indian migration. It is not that one can assume there has never been any anxiety in the West Indian immigrant's adjustment (including the inevitable acculturation). No part of even "normal" living is totally anxiety free. The point is that it should not be assumed a priori that excessive or abnormal anxiety is present. For instance, Srole, Langner, Michael, Opler, and Rennie (1962) spoke of a "historically realistic" anxiety among Jews. Raised in an "exilic environment," the Jewish family acted to condition the progeny—acted as a prophylactic, that is—against the more severe pressure and traumas of constant migration (p. 308). One can rightfully hypothesize a not dissimilar historically realistic (that is, nonpathological) level of anxiety among Caribbean immigrants to the United States, to Europe, and to other Caribbean countries.

One could point to the specific case of the Barbadians Wright was so concerned about. Their successes as skilled workers were well-known in the other West Indian islands where they were often contracted as police officers, teachers, and magistrates. However, it was their role in the construction of the Panama Canal at the turn of the century that made them legendary as adaptable people even in the midst of brutal working conditions, gross racism, and discriminatory practices (Lewis, 1975; Mack, 1944; Maloney, 1989). In Panama, Barbadians represented 44.1% of the total workforce during the construction years (1904 to 1914), and this in turn represented 40% of all the adult men of Barbados. They came semiskilled and semiliterate but never stagnated in their jobs. McCullough (1977) said "Whatever his first job ... , the Black worker was not likely to stay with it very long ... some change in his own circumstances seemed always to lead to something more attractive" (p. 580). They later moved up the Central American coast, building railroads and docks, and opening up banana plantations, all with similar successes as immigrants in general, and as skilled workers in particular.

However, West Indian success has not been limited to migration to Commonwealth countries or Panama. It is also a matter of record in the United States, even while that country was riddled with racist attitudes and practices. The West Indians' successful navigation of U.S. society is legendary. As Foner (1979) recorded, in 1970 the highest ranking Blacks in New York's police department were all West Indians. All Black federal judges in the city, as well as successive borough presidents of Manhattan, were West Indians (Foner, 1979, pp. 285–287). Sowell (1981) explained that even as West Indians remained "socially distinct" from Black Americans, their success could be explained by their ability to "represent" the larger Black community generally and in particular to relate to the White community (p. 216). As Sowell noted: "To stress their specifically West Indian background would undermine their positions with Blacks and Whites alike" (p. 220).

New scholarship now reveals that even those most "invisible" of the West Indian migrants, women, had "achievements, abilities, and attitudes ... quite admirable by American standards" (Mortimer & Bryce-Laporte, 1981, p. xiv). Research also shows West Indians, whether in New York, Miami, or Toronto, mobilizing politically and culturally as West Indians. Their successful integration and, yes, manipulation and capacity to "play" the dominant cultures and societies did not reduce their sense of national identity. There are lessons in this for this age of globalization.

GLOBALIZATION AND MULTIPLE IDENTITIES?

This historical West Indian success as migrants puts into focus the newfound theme of migration in a globalized world. Castles and Miller (1988) noted that there will be increasing numbers of migrants and that they have loyalties to more than one society. They asserted that because dual and multiple citizenship will become increasingly common among migrants, one can speak of "multiple identities, [and this will] bring into question prevailing notions of the nation-state and citizenship" (p. 16). They were hardly pessimistic on that score: "It is part of the migrant condition, [they wrote] to develop multiple identities, which are linked to the cultures both of the homeland and to the country of origin. ... Such personal identities possess complex new transcultural elements" (p. 16). Their hope is shared by Fishman (1985), that the globalization of migration will lead to reduced nationalism and increased unity worldwide.

There are several problems with this approach. First, it assumes that what they call *identities* are all of equal weight and import in determining individual and collective behavior. Especially dangerous is the propensity to believe that the forces of globalization have eroded the sentiments of national identity. The experiences of the West Indian, both at home and before he migrated, demonstrate why.

No student of the independence and decolonization processes of the 1960s and 1970s doubted the strength of national identities. What they might have overlooked is how old and established these forces were in the islands. The strength of island parochialism, or more charitably, the tenacity of local feelings, dates way back to the early 19th century. As one 19th-century British governor, attempting to explain the failure of all attempts at federating some of the small islands, put it: "The islands, small and insignificant as they may be ... have kept up among their ruling classes a spirit of self-importance and narrow patriotism which may seem ludicrous but cannot be ignored" (Wrong, 1923, p. 148). If this narrow patriotism was true in the 19th century, it was even more so in the 20th. An American geographer who was skeptical of the ultimate success of the British idea of a West Indies Federation noted in 1960 (one year before its collapse) that each island was so jealous of the other that conflicting stereotypes and self-images governed inter-island relations. "Physical insularity, [he said] not only aggravates inter-island differences; it also intensifies a sense of belonging within each island, whatever its size" (Lowenthal, 1961, p. 68).

In the Caribbean, each island has been a nation for a long time. That unit became the unrivaled center of popular loyalties and sentiments. "Autonomy, unity and identity," according to Hutchinson and Smith (1994, p. 5), are the three themes and ideals that have been pursued by nationalists everywhere since they were popularized in Western and Central Europe in the 18th and 19th centuries. They have been alive and well in the Caribbean for a long time, often out of sight because of the ethnic and communal sentiments that seemed, and seem, to be overwhelming. They are not. National identity, above all other allegiances, has long represented the amalgam of political, cultural, and ethnic affiliations. It has been so recognized by an array of scholars, as Isaacs (1975) acknowledged. It has especially been so in the islands defined by their sea borders. This identity based on a finite piece of land surrounded by sea and divided from others by that sea is a formidable form of national identity. This is why Conner (1978) insisted on distinguishing between group affiliations, which are other *defined*, and the nation, which is *self-defined*. This self-definition is based on a national psychology: a subconscious belief in the group's separate origin. So powerful is this identity, said Hechter (2000, p. 94), that it is the only one for which people are liable to make ultimate sacrifices. It overrides all other allegiances. Geertz (1963) conveyed a similar opinion. Even as new states are:

> abnormally susceptible to serious disaffections based on primordial ethnic attachments to language, religion, race, region, in the final analysis all these allegiances have one aim: a search for an "identity" and that identity finds self-standing in one "maximal unit": the nation. (p. 110)

Here, again, the older social science literature is conceptually useful in explaining how and why steady national identities can emerge in socially plural and highly differentiated societies such as the West Indies even as they hone their ability to perform in different roles and social contexts, and operate in different social meanings. "The ability of the individual to alternate between these different settings," said Newman (1973), "is a prerequisite for living in [plural societies]" (p. 293).

And so, to return to Lamming's (1953) *In the Castle of My Skin,* it should come as no surprise that the setting for the protagonist's proclamation of a new allegiance toward his oppressed brothers in the United States is a rum shop. Listening to Paul Robeson belt out "Let My People Go," Trumper has expanded his set of allegiances; it now includes "the Negro race." It was incorrect, however, for Wright or anyone else to conclude from that extension of allegiances that Trumper had been seeking to substitute his national identity as a Barbadian. He was not seeking to be someone else, as Naipaul would have us believe. As the behavior of Caribbean diaspora have demonstrated over the years, their island national identities remain strong, emotionally and functionally. So does their capacity to play the part, whether holding their own in a rum shop-like context or making dramatic pronouncements of allegiance with oppressed groups elsewhere. This distinction between a historical and firmly held national identity and a facile capacity to multiply one's allegiances needs conceptual clarification.

CONCLUSIONS: ATTEMPTING CONCEPTUAL CLARITY

On the basic methodological principle that concepts (as distinct from hypotheses or theories) are not to be held as true or false, but rather as useful or not useful, the following is offered as an attempt at conceptual clarification.

If we retake the point made by Burton (1997) that West Indians borrow, adapt, and imitate, not as deference or subordination (much less self-hatred), but to maximize the possible gains from that imitation, we have partly answered the question as to why they have been such successful migrants. They know how to play the game at home and abroad even as they hold on to their national identities. Playing the game is similar to what Dashefsky (1972; Dashefsky & Shapiro, 1974) long ago termed an ability to engage in *multiple identifications*. To *identify* is to link oneself organizationally, as in becoming a member, and/or symbolically, as in thinking of oneself as part of a particular group or movement. Identifications are self-consciously goal-oriented (i.e., deliberate and instrumental), and an individual can clearly hold on to multiple such identifications. Identity, as in the sense of national identity outlined previously, is more deeply rooted. It is, as Smith (1991) maintained, "the most fundamental and inclusive" of all senses of belonging (p. 143). As Dashefsky (1972) explained—drawing heavily on Erikson and Goffman—it is that sector of the personal system that "maintains personal continuity through the coherent organization of information about the individual" (p. 242).

It is the individual's life history that tends to be the lasting influence. It is Lamming's (1953) autobiographical linking of Trumper's (i.e., Lamming's) life with that of Barbados, the nation he is about to leave, which is so poignant about his story. His national identity is clearly solidified; he is ready to migrate and play the game, whatever game his new environment demands.

It is not that such individuals always enjoy the performances they see fit to give or the identifications in which they have to engage. However, for those who have a strong sense of in-group solidarity such as that which exists in national identity and who, in addition, have a sense of gamesmanship—even humor—it is possible to learn to tolerate and derive personal advantages from the less-than-enjoyable roles. As Newman (1973) said, "Far from being a schizophrenic handicap, the challenge of multiple realities becomes a playing field for the expression of the diversity and freedom of the human condition" (p. 293).

The ability of West Indians to have multiple identifications, to play the field yet sustain a strong personal, participatory national identity shows that in their own way they have achieved that freedom of the human condition. And, not trivially, this freedom is a double-edged sword. On the positive side, it reverts to their personal benefits and through that to real benefits to their islands. Evidence of such benefits are the steady flow of remittances and the money-spending tourism to the home country. On the negative side is the continued insularity and parochialism that prevents broader alliances of an enduring political type. Although good at coalescing for specific tactical and strategic ends, each island remains a nation. The hope for a West Indian nation is as remote as it ever was.

REFERENCES

Abrahams, R. D. (1983). *The man of words in the West Indies. Performance and the emergence of Creole culture*. Baltimore: Johns Hopkins University Press.
Berry, J. W. (1980). Social and cultural change. In H. C. Triandis & R. W. Brislin (Eds.), *Handbook of cross-cultural psychology: Vol. 5. Social psychology* (pp. 211–279). Boston: Allyn and Bacon.
Burton, R. E. (1997). *Afro-Creole: Power, opposition and play in the Caribbean*. Ithaca, NY: Cornell University Press.
Castles, S., & Miller, M. J. (1988). *The age of migration* (2nd ed.). London: Macmillan.
Conner, W. (1978). A nation is a nation. *Ethnic and Racial Studies, 1*, 379–388.
Coser, L. A. (1977). *Masters of sociological thought*. New York: Harcourt Brace.
Dashefsky, A. (1972). And the search goes on: The meaning of religion-ethnic identity and identification. *Sociological Analysis, 33*.
Dashefsky, A., & Shapiro, H. M. (1974). *Ethnic identification among American Jews: Socialization and social structure*. Lexington, MA: Lexington.
Fishman, J. A. (1985). *The rise and fall of the ethnic revival: Perspective on language and ethnicity*. New York: Mouton.
Foner, N. (1979, Summer). West Indians in New York City and London: A comparative analysis. *International Migration Review*, 285–287.
Geertz, C. (1963). The integrative revolution: Primordial sentiments and civil politics in new states. In C. Geertz (Ed.), *Old societies and new states* (pp. 107–113). New York: Free Press.
Goffman, E. (1959). *The presentation of self in everyday life*. Garden City, NY: Doubleday.
Hechter, M. (2000). *Containing nationalism*. Oxford, England: Oxford University Press.
Hutchinson, J., & Smith, A. D. (Eds.). (1994). *Nationalism*. Oxford, England: Oxford University Press.
Isaacs, H. R. (1975). *Idols of the tribe: Group identity and political change*. New York: Harper & Row.
Kurokawa, M. (Ed.). (1970). *Minority responses*. New York: Random House.
Lamming, G. (1953). *In the castle of my skin*. New York: McGraw-Hill.
Lewis, L. S. (1975). *The West Indian in Panamá, 1850–1914*. Unpublished doctoral dissertation, Tulane University, New Orleans, LA.
Lowenthal, D. (Ed.). (1961). *The West Indies federation. Perspectives on a new nation*. New York: Columbia University Press.
Mack, G. (1944). *The land divided: A history of the Panamá canal and other isthmian canal projects*. New York: Knopf.

Maloney, G. (1989). *El Canal de Panamá y los trabajadores antillanos*. Panamá: Imprenta Universitaria.
McCullough, D. (1977). *The path between the seas: The creation of the Panamá Canal*. New York: Simon & Schuster.
Mortimer, D. M., & Bryce-Laporte, R. S. (Eds.). (1981). *Female immigrants to the United States: Caribbean, Latin American and African experiences* (RIIES Occasional Papers No. 2). Washington, DC: Smithsonian Institution.
Naipaul, V. S. (1967). *The mimic men*. London: Deutsch.
Naipaul, V. S. (1972). *The overcrowded barracoon*. London: Deutsch.
Newman, W. M. (1973). *American pluralism*. New York: Harper & Row.
Parrillo, W. M. (2000). *Strangers to these shores* (6th ed.). Boston: Allyn and Bacon.
Patterson, O. (1978). Migration in Caribbean societies. In W. H. McNeill & R. S. Adams (Eds.), *Human migration* (pp. 106–145). Bloomington: Indiana University Press.
Sanua, V. D. (1980). Familiar and sociocultural antecedents of psychopathology. In H. C. Triandis & J. G. Draguns, *Handbook of cross-cultural psychology: Vol. 6. Psychopathology* (pp. 175–236). Boston: Allyn and Bacon.
Smith, A. D. (1991). *National identity*. Reno: University of Nevada Press.
Sowell, T. (1981). *Ethnic America: A history*. New York: Basic.
Srole, L., Langner, T. S., Michael, S. T., Opler, M. K., & Rennie, F. A. C. (1962*). Mental health in the metropolis: The midtown Manhattan study*. New York: McGraw-Hill.
Wrong, H. (1923). *Government of the West Indies*. Oxford, England: Clarendon.

Racial Politics and Cultural Identity in Trinidad's Carnival

Amanda Lynn Zavitz
Anton L. Allahar
Department of Sociology
University of Western Ontario

The tendency to essentialization is common in so-called diaspora studies and their explicit acceptance of primordially based identity politics. In this critique of the volume edited by Smart and Nehusi (2000), we focus on the authors' references to Africa and Africans, and on their uncritical use of such notions as community, race, and ethnicity. The authors speak ideologically to what supposedly binds the community together; for example, common blood lines, common ethnocultural experience, common collective memory, common African origins, and so on. We say *supposedly*, for much of this idea of community cohesiveness is rather mythical or fictional. It is part of the essentialization and homogenization of Africa and Africans, and in the process, such studies do not highlight those social and structural features that divide the community. This is a common theme in diaspora studies that, whether wittingly or unwittingly, serves to legitimate the illegitimate concept of race.

In this article we seek to clarify one aspect in the definition of the term *cultural identity*. It is our intention to problematize the political dimensions of the term as it applies to the Trinidad Carnival. We also wish to examine the implications for those who, given the present understanding of the term, are defined out of the societal culture. As will be seen, there are some commentators (Smart & Nehusi, 2000) who have equated the Carnival with the country's national festival, and who have insisted that the Carnival is an African cultural product belonging entirely to Africans.

Such an approach, which draws heavily on the idea that ethnoracial attachments are primordial (Allahar, 1996), serves very clear political ends. It also implies that the so-called Indian Trinidadians, who, for whatever reason, do not see Carnival as their national cultural marker, are denied a place to call home:

Requests for reprints should be sent to Anton L. Allahar, Department of Sociology, University of Western Ontario, London, Ontario, Canada N6A 5C2. E-mail: allahar@uwo.ca

> For Caribbean people and many others, the ultimate representation of home is carnival ... we know that we will be understood there. It is the dwelling place of some of our deepest affections; the place of familiarity and of family that reminds us of the ancestors because of the material markers of their presence there. (Nehusi, 2000a, p. 1)

For both Smart and Nehusi (2000), the terms *Black* and *African* are loosely treated as synonyms, and as will be seen, Nehusi's use of the term *Caribbean people* in the aforementioned quotation is meant to signify "Black" or African-descended people.

Although there are many Indian Trinidadians who participate in the Carnival and many who do not, there are also many African Trinidadians who participate and many who do not. This notwithstanding, several commentators continue to see the annual Carnival as Trinidad's national festival and the country's flagship cultural event. As early as 1972, for example, Hill (1972) saw in the Carnival the potential for developing a *national* theater, and the recent contributions of Peter Minshall's *mas* bands, among others, have gone a long way in making that potential seem even more real. In the minds of Black nationalists, however, the "national festival" that is Carnival is racialized and has become synonymous with African history and traditions. In other words, the Carnival, which was born in Africa, is the supreme African festival and belongs entirely to Black people (Smart & Nehusi, 2000); who, regardless of where they were born, are Africans! Africa is *home* for all Africans. For his part, Smart (2000a) depicted the Trinidad Carnival as "the quintessential African festival" (p. 72). And in the estimation of another observer, Nehusi (2000b), the street parade segment of the celebration is symbolic of the Africans' reclaiming their physical, spiritual, and cultural freedom: "Possession of the streets was a sign of Afrikan possession of self, a spiritual reconnection with ancestors through millennia of cultural practice, a liberation through expression of impulses carried in genes for uncounted generations" (p. 96).

It is our contention that the foregoing constitutes only part of the larger racist agenda of those Black nationalists who want to define Carnival in racial terms (Allahar, 1998). Thus, Smart (2000a) declared: "Trinbagonians can then rightly claim their festival as 'we thing' only because it is a 'black thing'" (p. 72). The loose invoking of the royal *we* must not be taken as referring to all Trinbagonians, for as this article makes evident, Smart has a very definite idea of who "we" is and of what *Black* means. The intention is clearly one of racial inclusion and exclusion, for those who are not defined as Black, which in this context means African, are not part of "we."

As our article makes clear, the message is not all that complicated, nor, at the same time, is it free of contradiction. For example, going back to Nehusi's (2000b, p. 96) previously discussed comment, little did he realize the racist implications of claiming that behavior, whether economic, political, cultural, or social, is genetically coded! This is the kind of statement one expects from Nazis, members of the Ku Klux Klan, and assorted other racists designated as White, Black, Brown, Yellow, Red, and other. It also smacks of the same kind of essentialism, if not racism, reflected in Smart's (2000a) declaration that "the African mind is one that deals with the big picture. The African mind is driven by and towards holism" (p. 51). It would seem as though there is some secret that the African mind alone has been able to uncover, and also that all Africans are possessed of this special gift.

THE MYTH OF HOME

In a recent doctoral dissertation on the political and racial underpinnings of the military coups in Fiji, Halapua (2001) charged that the problems of contemporary Fiji are due almost entirely to the country's colonial past and the perverse designs of the evil colonials, mainly White, British administrators. In a manner reminiscent of those who propagated the myth of a merry Africa—according to which all Africans in Africa loved one another and got along beautifully before the advent of the White slave masters—the author of the dissertation invoked the notion of *vanua* in Fiji. *Vanua* is a loosely defined, almost religious spirit of oneness that supposedly united all Fijians in times of precolonial contact. It is a romantic view of Fijian society that promises to transcend all divisions of class, tribe, ethnicity, sex, and region, and according to the author, if the current problems of the country are to be overcome, the spirit of *vanua* must be rediscovered. His is a plea for going back home, for taking the country back from the foreigners who invaded it, and restoring the culture that emphasized oneness with nature, with the land, and with one's fellows: *vanua*.

In the same sense, the contributors to the recent volume entitled *Ah Come Back Home: Perspectives on the Trinidad and Tobago Carnival* (Smart & Nehusi, 2000) can be seen as endorsing the myth of merry Africa and spinning tall tales of racial identity and solidarity among Africans the world over. Smart and Nehusi, the editors of this volume, are unequivocal in their claim that Africa is the cradle of human civilization and the source of ancient human history. To their mind, contemporary history was written and produced by White supremacist barbarians bent on denigrating the signal contributions of Africans (Nehusi, 2000a; Smart, 2000a). This theme was also picked up by other contributors to the volume. Thus, Alleyne-Dettmers (2000, p. 139) essentialized "barbaric Europeans," and both Smart (2000b) and Moran (2000) condemned what they referred to generally as "European barbarism," while Adeyinka (2000, p. 111) spoke more specifically of the "heroic struggles of Africans" to liberate themselves "from Spanish, French and British barbarism." Adeyinka went on to rail against the White supremacist system, just as Nehusi (2000a, p. 13) spoke of the "white racist authorities," and Moran (2000, p. 174) of what the "white supremacist system" has done to African Americans, forcibly alienating and separating those in the United States from their sisters and brothers in the rest of the Americas.

Moran (2000) wanted to rewrite history from an Afrocentric point of view and in the process made some truly outrageous claims. For example, she charged that

"Africans formulated the major theological tenets of Christianity thousands of years ago, but Christianity is considered by all to be a white man's religion" (p. 175). And thinking specifically of the Trinidad Carnival, she saw this as a conspiracy on the part of what she calls "white bandits [and those] Aryan marauders ... the vast hordes of starving Aryan barbarians" (p. 175); who, even today, would steal "we thing," which is Carnival and steel band! However, as noted previously, to the extent that *we* is African, it does not include those non-African segments of the Trinidadian population. It is the same unspecified use of the word *we* by Martin (2000), who, when speaking of Carnival in the diaspora, referred to "this thing *we* call, mas, *we* thing, *we* Carnival [italics added]" (p. 180). Similarly, where syntax demands, the personal pronoun *our* is interchanged with the royal *we*. Thus, Smart (2000a), who appeared uncomfortable with the traditional idea of White tourism from North America and Europe to the Caribbean, eschewed any attempt at class analysis, and charged: "After all it is *our* sun, and *our* sea, and *our* sex and *our* fun [italics added] that those hungry visitors from the North come seeking" (p. 36).

As with the *we* discussed earlier, there is no attempt to specify just who *our* refers to. Is it all Trinidadians, or all Africans, or what Smart (2000a, 2000b), Alleyne-Dettmers (2000), and Moran (2000) termed *African-ancestored* Trinidadians? And just how does one go about defining *African* in Trinidad? Do we use the same racist criteria as the Nazis and the Ku Klux Klan: skin color, hair texture, nose shape, and penis size? In a system of widespread "race" mixing, are so-called African-ancestored people not also simultaneously European ancestored, Indian ancestored, and so on? On what basis, then, does one privilege the African over the other elements? Such an uncritical understanding of the term *Trinidadian* makes sense to us. For, above all else, the term signifies a rich, historical, and ethnocultural mixture of a polyglot people. That rich mixture should therefore be the necessary starting point for any discussion of who or what constitutes a true, true Trini.

EUROCENTRICITY AND AFROCENTRICITY

To this end, Afrocentricity constitutes an obstacle, and is blinding even to the very contributors to *Ah Come Back Home* (Smart & Nehusi, 2000). We all know that in no system of logic do two wrongs make a right. Thus, if in principle Eurocentricity is wrong, how, in principle, can Afrocentricity be right? Springer (2000), the director of Trinidad's National Heritage Library, seemed to think that there is no contradiction to be found in the condemnation of Eurocentricity and the simultaneous promotion of Afrocentricity. Thus, she declared that Trinidad's "society needs really to lose its hatred and fear of the word African and of Afrocentricity" (p. 25). The contradictions also mount when she wrote of her own participation in the 1970 Carnival street parade, which coincided that year with the Black Power disturbances in Trinidad. Here she wrote: "We marched and pranced to the music of the African drums. No tourists joined that band" (p. 23). In the same paragraph she noted that all the revolutionary icons were present in the same band, which supposedly featured no tourists, "from Ché Guevara to our own Kwame Turé, from Huey Newton to Malcolm X" (p. 23). One is left to wonder whether she was aware of the fact that Ché was a White man from Argentina, or that both Huey Newton and Malcolm X, if they were to attend the Carnival in the flesh, would have had to be issued tourist visas!

Echoing Nehusi's (2000a) sentiments to the effect that today "there is no major Afrikan band leader in Trinidad" (p. 11), Springer (2000) went on to lament the passing of George Bailey—in her words, the last great African band leader in the country. She pointed out that Trinidad and Tobago's Carnival "today boasts not one substantial African bandleader of charisma and creativity. ... Rather, we have the situation of African people flocking to play mas with Peter Minshall" (p. 18). What Springer was saying is that she had a formula for determining who is an African in Trinidad. And like any common or garden-variety racist she knew that George Bailey was an African, and that Peter Minshall, whom Smart (2000a, p. 74) described as "a white Trinidadian," is not. One can surmise only that Wayne Berkeley was eliminated owing to lack of "substance." In Springer's estimation, other light-skinned Trinidadian bandleaders such as the late Edmund Hart and Harold Saldenah, or even the Chinese Trinidadian Stephen Leung and the Indian Trinidadian Raoul Garib had no African *ancestry,* and even if they are "substantial bandleaders" they do not qualify, for they are not "African," and hence, do not really have any authentic claim on the Carnival.

In the foregoing we choose to specify the term *ancestry* as opposed to *blood* for two reasons: (a) we are fully convinced that the concept of biological race, particularly in sociological analysis, is utterly meaningless, and (b) the U.S. racist *law of hypodescent,* according to which one drop of Black blood makes one Black, is entirely offensive to us, not to mention nonsensical and antiscientific. For we all know that in color terms blood is neither white nor black!

However, there is more by way of essentialization and contradiction to be drawn out of the Black nationalist position. For all the African purity that is claimed by the contributors to the aforementioned volume, and their simultaneous rejection of things European, Smart and Nehusi (2000) seemed most comfortable writing the dedication of their book in Latin—*In Memoriam* and *Requiescant In Pace*—and then Smart (2000a, pp. 30–31) quite gratuitously insisted on using the Latin *nunc* twice in place of a simple *now* when trying to capture the dynamic fluidity of the present.

ESSENTIALIZATION OF AFRICA AND AFRICANS

When Moran (2000) affirmed: "It cannot be overstated that we, Africans, invented civilization" (p. 174), it is clear she made no distinction between or among Africans from the North, South, West, East, or even central parts of that vast continent. This essentializing of the Africans as comprising a single, undifferentiated community is also evident in a second piece by Smart (2000b) in the same volume, where he wrote that "Africans all over the globe who have been subjected to white supremacy must be engaged unremittingly in the struggle for liberation in order to be made whole again" (p. 199). It is clear that he was not referring to only Africans in Africa, but also to Black people all over the world who choose to claim some African ancestry.

The tendency to essentialization is common in so-called diaspora studies and their explicit acceptance of primordially based identity politics (Allahar, 1996). In this case, references to Africa and Africans use the notions of community, race, and ethnicity as their main units of analysis. The authors of the studies contained in Smart and Nehusi (2000) spoke ideologically to what supposedly binds the community together; for example, common blood lines, common ethnocultural experience, common collective memory, common African origins, and so on.

We say *supposedly*, for much of this idea of community cohesiveness is rather mythical or fictional. It is part of the essentialization of Africa and Africans to which we have alluded. In the move to homogenize and essentialize Africans, diaspora studies do not highlight those social and structural features that divide the community. We are thinking here of internal, class, color, economic, and political inequalities within, say, the so-called African diasporic community, not to mention ideological cleavages related to religion and inter- and intraethnic rivalries. These divisions are real but are generally masked by sentimental and ideological appeals to a diasporic unity and identity in which coethnic brothers and sisters are easily accepting of one another. Also, by masking internal divisions, diaspora studies can be seen as promoting fear, mistrust, and even hostility toward those who are outside the community: the Other.

Such studies, and those who promote them, deliberately revise certain historical facts, such as the capture and sale of Africans by Africans to slave traders, ethnic cleansing within the "Black" communities of Rwanda and Burundi, or Black-on-Black violence within the African American community. For these reasons, it is easy to see why any facile appeal to community cohesion on the basis of race is unlikely to withstand critical scrutiny. Hence our skepticism. In other words, whether we are dealing with economic entrepreneurs of the business sector, who use race to divide workers and pay low wages, or with political and ethnic entrepreneurs, who seek to promote the idea of community cohesion along lines of common race, color, and culture, the ideological functions of political distraction and social control are unmistakable.

In sum, then, the primordial argument is troubling, for it seeks to essentialize Africa and Africans. We all know that Africa is a continent and not a country, and we also know that African societies and peoples vary widely among themselves in terms of phenotype, culture, social structure, political institutions, systems of religious belief, economic practices, and so on. And to this we must also add that African countries, like those of the West, are deeply internally divided along lines of class, economics, politics, ethnicity, and all the other lines that we are so familiar with in the West generally. So when we speak of the African diaspora, precisely to what Africa, or African country, or African culture, or African people are we referring? The idea that one can identify an African diaspora, which transcends the divisions of which we have spoken, and implies class and political consensus and fraternal goodwill, just does not square with reality. To our minds, such a notion of diaspora is ideological, and it tends to beg more questions than it answers.

COMMUNITY COHESION?

A central theme in diaspora studies is that of the "community in exile," whether voluntary or involuntary, and its links with the "community of origin," in this case, a place called Africa. Without making itself too explicit, this theme in diaspora studies invokes the idea of race and biology as rooted in common geography. The community of origin, for example, is Mother Africa, and Africans in the diaspora are connected to Mother by myths of shared ancestry, history, culture, lived experience, and sometimes even psychology.

This is directly linked to the idea of primordialism, which holds that human beings are yoked to their communities of origin by ties of blood that are natural, automatic, and unnecessary to articulate, and that require no explanation (Allahar, 1994, 1996). Those ties just exist, plain and simple. Although we do not wish to belittle what to some is a real sense of belonging or attachment to their community of origin, it is not entirely clear just what constitutes that community. Is it a geographic space? Is it a biologically discrete group? Or is it a culturally, and hence socially, constructed concept that might be more imagined than real? If it is socially constructed, what might be the motives and interests of the constructors?

In our approach to the question, we prefer to see diasporic and primordial identities as heavily socially imagined and constructed on myths of common descent and ancestry, which treat the community in question as a homogeneous, undifferentiated entity (Smart & Nehusi, 2000). Serious internal division and difference, especially those based on class, are creatively imagined away. And it is in this psychological sense that the idea of primordial attachment and belonging becomes so appealing to those who feel displaced and threatened, those whose powerlessness conspires to render them invisible and inefficacious.

This is the context in which we find the concept of the African diaspora somewhat troubling. For all too often its fictional and socially constructed aspects are unrecognized, and one is left to speculate at the motives of those entrepreneurs, ethnic and otherwise, who are so bent on promoting the fiction: Cornell West in academia, Spike Lee in entertainment, Louis Farrakhan in religion, Smart and Nehusi in popular culture. For example, it is commonly heard—and not incorrectly at that—that generally speaking, African Americans and African

Trinidadians know little of Africa, its histories, geographies, languages, and cultures, and even its politics. Wherein, then, lies the claim to be African anything? What does being African mean?

To the extent that it (Africa) is largely a place of psychological escape (and nothing is wrong with that), we think it is important that this be recognized and openly acknowledged. That this is not commonly acknowledged is troubling. Far too many commentators act as if this vision of Africa were an uncomplicated and undifferentiated empirical reality, and their calls to "action" are based on erroneous assumptions.

Although African traditions and heritage are a part of Carnival, this does not mean that Carnival is an exclusively African tradition. Yet, this is not the interpretation or perception that many people within Trinidad and Tobago, as well as tourists who visit, seem to hold. In this regard, Indian Trinidadians have traditionally been seen as out of place, even as intruders in the Carnival experience. This image of the Indian "invader" is not only held by some African participants and spectators of Carnival, but has also been internalized by segments of the Indian population. In a society as ethnically divided as Trinidad, this lack of participation by some East Indians in Carnival festivities has interesting and important social implications that are tied to national identity and also mirror the larger ethnic politics of the country. We turn now to an examination of this point.

WHAT DOES IT MEAN TO ASSERT THAT CARNIVAL IS AN "AFRICAN" TRADITION?

Greene (1974) emphasized the social conception of race in the Caribbean in that it goes beyond strict biological criteria. In Trinidad and Tobago, moreover, the official colonial census has "allowed" respondents to categorize themselves into "White, East Indian, African, Mixed, Syrian, Lebanese, or Chinese," (Burton, 1997, p. 157) for racial classification. However, in this article, the concern is not what anthropologists think or mean by *race*, but what the people of Trinidad and Tobago think when they use the word, not only in their daily lives, but specifically in the context of Carnival.

In Trinidad, race and ethnicity permeate all of the society's social, cultural, political, and economic institutions and practices because they are implicated in the power struggles of everyday life (Yelvington, 1993). Within this context, race is assumed to be biological, fixed, or immutable so that any attempt to treat it as a social construction is resisted vigorously by those who have a great deal of emotion invested in notions of racial purity and associated concepts of cultural superiority (Allahar, 1996). However, we argue that race is not real, but rather is a social-psychological construct or measure used to categorize groups of people who feel themselves to be similar in nature. Once set, those categories have very real consequences for the groups and individuals concerned.

The historical legacies of slavery and indentureship in Trinidad and Tobago have conditioned a multicultural society wherein social and political statuses are related to race, color, and culture. Although the advent of the global age has witnessed a weakening of these divisions, they persist in certain quarters and are fueled by ethnic entrepreneurs of all groups. Thus, in the contemporary context, to be an African has two possible meanings. The first is legalistic: One is a citizen of an African country. The second is socially constructed, primordial, or biological: One's origin or history might be tied to Africa, yet one is not a citizen.

Because it is highly uncommon for a Trinidadian to hold citizenship of an African country, it is the latter meaning of *African* to which we wish to turn: the question of origins. We argue that the biological aspects of these origins are far less important or salient than the emotional sense of belonging to Africa. Thus, to be African in Trinidad is a socioemotional choice that is heavily steeped in identity politics. Furthermore, in an age where a first-come, first-served definition of ownership is generally accepted, even when it comes to the ownership of such intangible things as culture and identity, the African Trinidadian is seen to have a greater claim to the nation's patrimony than his or her Indian, Chinese, or Syrian counterparts, who arrived later (Burton, 1997).

To be African in Trinidad is not to have some gene or blood type or even a certain shade of "blackness." Instead, it is to identify oneself, and to be identified by others, as such. Moreover, it is a perception of self as tied to a community of other people; a sense of kinship based on perceptions of similarity—specifically, of coming from the same background and sociohistorical circumstances. Certain symbols such as body type, skin color, and hair texture are adopted for use in specific circumstances to indicate "groupness."

These symbols are available not just for any interpretation, but for the hegemonic interpretation advanced by the groups who hold political and economic power, and who are able to legitimate this power via the subjection of subordinated groups. In this context, narratives of the past are not neutral. Although the relationship of ethnicity to the past is multivocal, one determinant of this value is the position of the ethnic groups to the widely construed division of labor (see Mintz, 1981; Williams, 1960). This process of ethnic identity construction involves sensing likeness in a population historically characterized by a plurality of differences, and attaching meaning (and thus value) to those identities.

Part of this perception is also based on a comparison of self to the Other. In the case of African Trinidadians, historically, the Other has largely been the White Europeans who have dominated them, and the Indians, whom at some points in history they have dominated. Therefore, in a similar way that conceptualizations of being White have traditionally been formulated against the Black Other, African Trinidadianness is constructed against, and in relation to (among others), the East Indian Other, to whom African Trinidadians have at some points in history felt a sense of superiority, and whom at other points have perceived as a threat.

THE ENTRANCE OF EAST INDIANS
INTO TRINIDAD AND TOBAGO

The ownership and operation of sugar plantations provided the main bases for Trinidad's ethnocultural diversity. After the emancipation of the slaves, the planters in Trinidad were pressed to solve the resulting labor shortage. Thus, a system of indentured labor was invoked, with the result that between 1845 and 1917, when indentureship was ended, approximately 143,000 Indians were brought to the country. In 1921, Indians accounted for 33.18% of the total population (Deosaran, 1981). Apart from the social identification, religious affiliation in Trinidad is widely recognized as playing a significant role in intergroup relations (Jha, 1974; Malik, 1971; Samaroo, 1987; Williams, 1962). In relation to African Trinidadians, Indians cannot be understood simplistically as a homogenous ethnocultural group. Instead, lines of division among East Indians have been drawn in terms of class, political allegiance, locus of residence (rural vs. urban), and religion (Hindu vs. Muslim). As evidence of these intraethnic divisions, the People's National Movement Party, which played a decisive role in the politicization of Carnival, was perceived as a collaboration of African Trinidadians, and Christian and Muslim Indians, who were defined in opposition to the larger Hindu population and the small but influential Roman Catholic (popularly known as French Creole) population. Thus, in terms of social, political, and economic domination, the Indians historically have been divided.

Partly because of religious differentiation and partly because of racial, political, and economic sensitivity, the Indians, when introduced to the country, were received by the ex-slaves with a mixture of fear, contempt, and indifference, much of which was encouraged by the planters. In response, the Indians isolated themselves physically, occupationally, and culturally. Thus, African–Indian encounters have historically been characterized by separation and xenophobia. The two races did not mix. Instead, because neither group felt its existence to be threatened in any way by the other, they lived in uneasy, but mainly nonviolent coexistence (Brereton, 1975). Specifically,

> when the Indians began settling in the society, they did so on terms most unfavorable for themselves. Not only did they occupy the lowest-paid sector of the economy but they were also placed by other social groups in the lowest position in the system of social stratification operative in the society. (Singh, 1974, pp. 48–49)

Whereas in 1960 approximately 71% of the Indian population, as opposed to 44% of Africans, lived in rural Trinidad, where wages and opportunity for social integration were much lower, this difference was even greater by 1970 (Braithwaite & Crichlow, 1991; Deosaran, 1981; Ryan, 1991).

RACIALIZED CONSCIOUSNESS

Although 150 years have now passed and the Indians have achieved social, economic, and political mobility, traces of that isolation are still found. Specifically, prejudices and stereotypes that were developed by both groups toward one another during the colonial period are still strong today (Singh, 1974; Trotman, 1991). In a highly urbanized and industrialized society, however, Trinidadian Indians could not insulate themselves very effectively from the processes of Creolization that had early transformed their African compatriots. Indeed today, in an increasingly *dougla*-rized society, it seems as though the fundamental divisions are more fruitfully examined in terms of class rather than ethnicity or race.

Thus, along with the suggestion that carnival does not symbolize the entire Trinidadian nation is the racialization of political consciousness connected to its conceptualization. In discussing the racialization of consciousness in Trinidad and Tobago, Allahar (1998) spoke of the tendency for racial differences to be perceived as crucial in determining political actions, economic opportunities, social standing, even cultural legitimacy, or authenticity. Because this racialized consciousness has been fostered and is so highly developed in Trinidad and Tobago, there is a tendency to minimize the importance of class as an analytical concept for explaining social inequality.

Carnival is no exception to this rule. Rather, the class divisions, intricately tied to ideologies of race and cultural superiority in Trinidadian history, and have been played out in the history of Carnival, provide further evidence that it is not strictly an African tradition, but a reflection of the class and politics of the larger Trinidad society. To say that Carnival is more tied to Africanness, or African culture, is really to make the statement that the primary purpose of Carnival is to serve either as a point of primordial connection for Africans, or as an affirmation of this connection. Although this may be true on some level, in that African Trinidadians may "connect" or come together with one another during Carnival, we would argue that this is more an assertion of their historical and cultural connection to Trinidad than it is to Mother Africa. Stated differently, although Carnival is partly about the formulation and maintenance of primordial kinship or communal ties, it is less about affirming a sense of Africanness and more about affirming Trinidadianness, or more specifically, which social class has a stronger claim to the shaping of Trinidadian culture. The racialization of political consciousness surrounding Carnival is linked to the country's history, the terms and conditions under which the various groups of immigrants arrived, their relation to capital, their differential access to and use of power, and the various patterns of adaptation or resistance (Allahar, 1998).

A HISTORICAL REVIEW OF TRINIDADIAN CARNIVAL

Trinidad Carnival, Miller (1991) wrote, "seems to change its implications almost each decade, facing about to address different aspects of Trinidadian society such as emancipation, race, class, and gender" (p. 330). Historically, Carnival as a tradition in Trinidad can be divided into four main epochs or periods of cultural, economic, and political rule:

1. The elite preemancipation Carnival, the period from the Cedula of 1783 to full emancipation in 1838, when Carnival was originally established and dominated by the French planters and aristocrats;
2. The transitional phase of postemancipation Carnival—the *jamette* era—that extended from 1838 to 1884, in which ex-slaves played the most pivotal role;
3. The period from 1884 to 1941, when Carnival, without losing its rebellious potential, became steadily more "respectable" and began to evolve into a truly national festival;
4. The period of the "modern" Carnival from 1945 to present, characterized by increased ties to national ideology, commercialization, politicalization, and theatricalization.

Throughout each of these phases in Trinidadian history, Carnival has not been strictly an African event, but rather the "site of contestation and resistance to hegemonic formation" (Traube, 1996, p. 133).

Because inequalities of race, class, and cultural, political, and economic dominations of wider Trinidadian society were not only imposed, but also played out in Carnival, this produced tensions, contradictions, and ironies, all of which have left their mark on the festivities. Indeed, in this way, Carnival is a mirror, which historically has reflected the changing structures, social relations, and political and economic conditions of Trinidad and Tobago. Emancipation in the 19th century, the rise of a non-European educated middle class in the 19th century, and calls to nationalism and political independence in the 20th century have each had their impact not on "African" but on "Trinidadian" Carnival.

Thus, despite claims by Black nationalists, Carnival is not strictly about race. Instead, it has historically symbolized the constructs and confines of division and nationalism inherent in Trinidad as a nation. Although the trajectory of the Carnival has been punctuated by struggle, if Carnival is about the politics and economics of race and class conflict, it is also about accommodation between antagonistic groups in the society (Ho, 2000).

PREEMANCIPATION CARNIVAL

Carnival was originally introduced into Trinidad and Tobago not by Africans, but by French immigrants in the late 18th century. Trinidad had been an underdeveloped colony of Spain until the year 1793, when peace treaties were signed between Spain, France, and Britain, which resulted in a policy that strongly encouraged settlement by Roman Catholics (Anthony, 1989; Hill, 1972; Van Koningsbruggen, 1997). As a result, French aristocrats from other Caribbean colonies began to settle in Trinidad, bringing with them not only their slaves, but their Carnival traditions (Ho, 2000). On one hand this French version of Carnival was a festival of dance, music, song, and drama; on the other, it was a collective expression of the perceptions, meanings, aspirations, and struggles engendered by the material conditions of social life and informed by the cultural traditions of the group.

The French who settled in Trinidad, following the Cedula of Population in 1783, were distinguished by color and shade as well as class. Specifically, there were White planters and those of Color, slaves, and free persons of Color. During this period, the dominant class was made up of Whites, but not all Whites belonged to it. However, within their ranks, individuals were distinguished by nationality and religion so that a hierarchical order dominated by the planter elite, merchants, and government officials was formed. Because class mobility is so intricately tied to color, in that the whiter the skin the better socioeconomic position, the racial boundary between these elites and the rest of the population was virtually impenetrable, even by the wealthy planters of Color (Lee, 1991).

As De Freitas (1994) noted, two simultaneous, almost contradictory movements can be discerned in Trinidad during this period. On the one hand, there was separation on the basis of race, class, and color, intricately woven into Carnival celebrations and underpinned by the assertion of European culture's superiority over African culture. On the other hand, there was a fusion of aspects of these two cultures to produce an identifiable Creole culture. Conflict and symbiosis: The simultaneous operations of centrifugal and centripetal forces within the structure of social relations have resulted in attitudes of contradiction and ambivalence throughout the society and the Carnival mosaic. From the beginning, it was apparent that Carnival was not a single, monolithic event, but multiple, parallel celebrations, practiced by different social segments that were bound together not only by power relations, but by sexual, personal, and kinship ties (De Freitas, 1994).

POSTEMANCIPATION CARNIVAL CELEBRATIONS

The "people's" Carnival did not emerge until after the abolition of slavery, first appearing in 1839 as a celebration of emancipation. The mass entry of ex-slaves into Carnival after emancipation changed not only the color of the festival, but its tone and content as well. The significance of this era can be divided into three areas of contestation relevant to the argument that Carnival is historically, politically, and socially a reflection of larger Trinidad society. The first area is *Canboulay,* the second concerns the *jamette* bands, and the third speaks to the hybrid resulting from Indian, specifically Hindu Indian, resistance to cultural assimilation. In the context of this discussion, we are most concerned with the third of these: the hybrid perspectives, traditions, and reflections.

Cultural Hybridity and Class Conflict

In addition to the divide between Europeans and Africans, the large-scale immigration of indentured laborers and general workers from India, China, Africa, and other Caribbean islands (Cowley, 1996; De Freitas, 1994) added greater complexity to the cultural and linguistic hybridity already present in Trinidad. Specifically, the introduction of Indians via indentureship created shifting and contradictory alliances that crosscut race, culture, and class loyalties within the Carnival complex (Ho, 2000). Between the 1850s and the 1880s, Carnival was a negotiation between a multiplicity of races and classes, rather than a simple opposition between White society and Black or Brown masses (De Freitas, 1994).

In all of this, the upper classes acted to protect their interests by attempting not only to denounce, but to abolish the street Carnival while maintaining the elegant ballroom masquerades of the elite and middle classes. In an attempt to ensure order and control of the masses, and to impose cultural conformity, the British authorities banned forms of cultural expression that challenged or threatened the dominant cultural practices. Thus, they passed laws to censor music and outlaw drums, wakes, and other "African" events (Anthony, 1989; Brereton, 1975; Cowley, 1996). Whereas British officials opposed Carnival because of its supposedly violent nature, it was the French Creole elite who came to its defense because they saw the British attempt at censorship as an attack on French culture (Rohlehr, 1990). As a part of their defensive strategy, the French elite reentered the street celebration in an attempt to save Carnival (Stuempfle, 1995). Hence, the perceivable "seamless," White, upper class alliance was threatened by the political symbolism of Carnival. It was this class, not racial or ethnic divide, that opened the gates for the middle class traditions that are so evident in today's Carnival.

However, at the beginning of the 20th century Carnival had become a festival in which all classes took part, the class and color distinctions that pervaded the larger society continued to be clearly reflected:

> The social classes still kept apart. In the main, one group of revelers playing traditional masquerades would tramp through the streets chanting choruses to the tambour-bamboo and bottle and spoon orchestras. Another group of revelers led by their *chantwels,* and dancing to calypso ..., were drawn from the colored middle-class. Yet a third group parading on carriages and on flat-bed trucks dressed as pirates, gypsies, or harem damsels were from the high colored and white merchant classes. (Hill, 1985, p. 27)

Thus, Lee (1991) wrote that "it would not be an exaggeration to suggest at this time in Trinidad's history, there were two Carnivals" (p. 427). Although Whites were not part of the downtown Carnival, it was the Black and middle class Carnival that was the more popular and successful one. What is important in this context is not only that the White elites never regained their dominance in Carnival after retreating at the end of slavery, but also that Indian participation is not even mentioned as an issue.

Sandwiched between the White, upper class, uptown Carnival whose participants were driven around the savanna in lorries, and the Black, lower class, *jamette* Carnival staged in the streets of downtown Port of Spain, "the creole middle-class articulated these separate carnivals as participants, organizers, patrons, judges, and musicians" (De Freitas, 1994, p. 112). The middle class had always been ambivalent about Carnival; on one hand, they disapproved of the excesses associated with the *jamette* Carnival, while on the other, they opposed the right of the White "foreign" British government to suppress local culture (De Freitas, 1994). Equally paradoxical is that, at the same time that it was cut off from the elite, the Creole middle class sought to earn its respect and admiration (Van Koningsbruggen, 1997). Furthermore, although these middle class members shared blood ties with the Black lower class, they tried to distance themselves from it socially. It is these issues of irony, ambivalence, paradox, and complexity represented in the middle class conceptualization of Carnival from its inception that are most reflected in its contemporary manifestation.

CONTEMPORARY CARNIVAL AS SYMBOL OF TRINIDADIAN UNITY AND NATIONHOOD

Increasingly, Trinidadian Carnival has become commercialized, commodified, and politicized. Today many economic entrepreneurs make common cause with their political and cultural counterparts to define the festival. It is portrayed as an event in which making money, doing cultural politics, and having fun are mutually reinforcing or complementary activities. However, the agenda remains a nationalist one that is still steeped in politics and economics of race and class. In a curious twist, the politically racialized consciousness historically surrounding Carnival is hidden or "swept" underground so that the festival is not only sold as, but becomes for some people, the "national" symbol of Trinidadian unity within diversity. However, the overall purpose of this political agenda is couched not in race, but in class terms. Not only are the profits for this seemingly nationalist agenda tied to capitalism, but the ideology of Carnival as a national festival symbolizing Trinidadian "unity" serves to mask and distract from greater class inequalities, not only within Carnival, but within the larger society. Therefore, when class is added to the analysis, Carnival is not simplistically an "African" event, based on African culture and traditions, but is an event that signifies and is connected to Trinidad as a *nation* with a capitalist economic structure.

However, given the class and ethnic divisions inherited from Trinidad's colonial past, national unity is not a simple matter. Each of the ethnic groups held and continue to hold negative stereotypes of the other. Blacks were regarded by the planters, and later by the East Indians, as being lazy and irresponsible, as having a penchant for drinking and conspicuous consumption, and being prone to profligacy (Ryan, 1991). East Indians on the other hand, were seen by Blacks and others as being miserly, prone to domestic violence, acquiescent to authority, clannish, and "heathen" for not adopting "Western" religious and cultural practices. The East Indians were also stereotyped as "coolies" or "low-life" because they performed the agricultural work rejected by the Creoles (Trotman, 1991).

This pitting by capital of the two main groups against one another had the effect of lowering the price of labor and, ultimately, of dividing the two groups. These divisions are best understood as unintended consequences of the colonial process, which necessitated certain specific forms of control and daily routine. The servile populations, who were tremendously differentiated along class, race, ethnic, religious, and linguistic lines, in their own countries of origin, were made to submit to a common set of demands that in the beginning respected neither race nor national origin (Allahar, 1995). Once the two fractions of the working class were pitted racially against one another, attention was successfully diverted from the larger capitalist system and the inequalities it bred.

THE 1990S: INDIANS ON THE MARCH?

By the early to mid-1990s, as the old political order began to unravel, the Indian element in the society was set to come to political maturity. The general elections of 1995, which saw the unprecedented 17 to 17 tie between the former ruling People's National Movement (PNM) party and the opposition United National Congress (UNC), set the stage for the redefinition of ethnic politics in Trinidad and Tobago (Allahar, 1998). When the tie was resolved in favor of the UNC, a mood of ethnic sensitivity enveloped the country, and it was not long before it was reflected in the popular political imagination associated with Carnival (Allahar, 1998).

In the years leading up to the significant event of 1995, there were other important social and political changes taking place in the country. Among these was the country's progressive urbanization, which affected the traditionally rural Indian population far more than the non-Indian population. The shift in residential locus posed serious challenges to the African Trinidadians' entrenched views of their Indian Trinidadian counterparts. The spatial and cultural boundaries that minimized the interaction between the two groups and kept them locked in their respective "places" were disappearing. In addition, a number of social markers that African Trinidadians had traditionally used to identify Indians and their place in the social order seemed to be evaporating: the Indians' identifiable style of dress, distinctive names, specific occupations, particular foods and eating patterns, and especially the demeanor and behavior of Indian women.

These changes were publicly evident in Carnival festivities. Young, liberal-minded Trinidadians of East Indian descent, especially those of Hindu and Islamic faiths, began to exercise their "freedoms," and to lay public claims to Trinidadianness by defying generations of family-prescribed isolation and African-imposed marginalization, and by playing an increasingly visible role in the "national" festival: Carnival. The former East Indians have not only achieved greater social mobility and economic prosperity (Reddock, 1999), but have also transformed themselves from Indians to Indian Trinidadians (Eriksen, 1992). Increasingly, too, the embarrassment of claiming Carnival as a national festival that shuts out one half of the population is being alleviated. Thus, despite the resistance by Black nationalists who continue to represent Carnival as an exclusively African cultural phenomenon, the continued evolution and metamorphosis of Carnival seem to suggest otherwise. In fact, in the postindependence period in Trinidad, particularly under PNM leadership, East Indian involvement in the Carnival, both as producers and consumers of *mas,* calypso, and pan, has increased dramatically.

Given the long history of racial tensions between African and Indian Trinidadians, the emergence of *chutney soca* suggests further the integration of Indians into the world of calypso and Carnival. *Chutney* is secular music that sprang from the East Indian working-class communities (Mason, 1998). Traditionally performed at Hindu weddings and also at female-only gatherings, *chutney* features musicians that tend to be men, while the dancers are mostly women who walk the tightrope between sexy and sexual. Yet, East Indian youth have little patience with the *chutney* of their elders and have thus produced music fusing *chutney* and *soca.* Ho (2000) described *chutney soca* as "the lyrical equivalent of Soca set to the blend of Indian and African rhythms, with an emphasis on jam and wine" (p. 12).

The entry of Indians via the media of *chutney* music; the *chutney* monarch competition; male and female Indian performers of calypso and *soca;* African Trinidadian calypsonians utilizing Indian themes, subjects, and musical instruments such as the *Tasa* drum; whole sections of award-winning bands that portray the Trinidadianized Indian traditions; the fact that one of the top steel band arrangers in the nation is Indian (Jit Samaroo), as is one of the top band leaders (Raoul Garib); along with much else show that the Carnival today is fast becoming a national festival, which includes rather than excludes Indian participation (Ho, 2000; Puri, 1997; Reddock, 1999). Although their participation in Carnival has increased dramatically, Indian calypsonians identify themselves with names such as "Mighty Indian" and "Hindu Prince," as though to confirm their distinct cultural heritage. Thus, they are not *playing* Carnival on "African" terms, as previously suggested stereotypes might suppose. Rather, Indians have entered the Carnival scene on their own terms, incorporating traditions and practices that are important to their culture and heritage.

Although race and ethnic inequalities have long been central for those trying to explain and describe the complexities of the Carnival process, very few seem to be aware of the class dimension of Trinidad's Carnival. In this article, we tried to show that Trinidad's Carnival is best understood initially as a class project of European colonialism onto which later class concerns of the wider society were appended. In other words, the political culture of today's Carnival is a reflection of the larger class-based and racialized social reality, only part of which is captured by the Black nationalists. Thus, the apparent marginalization of Blacks in Carnival, the source of Black nationalist panic, is best seen not in terms of race, but rather in the economic transformations of the Carnival spectacle, which itself reflects changes in the national economic and value structures of materialism, consumerism, and capitalism. In the process, the small (poor) person, not necessarily the Black person, has been trampled by the Carnival machine, which is fueled by the blind pursuit of profit:

> Formerly, a mas player was a part of an organization which worked collectively to bring out the band. Time and labour were freely given. Often the masquerader saw to making his or her own costume, although the design may have been determined beforehand. As carnival bands grew bigger, and big businesses saw a chance to capitalize, this relationship broke down so that now costumes are no longer custom made, but must be purchased in small, medium, or large. (Johnson, 1984, p. 184)

It is a familiar story: Old traditions and structures of social organizations are broken down as capitalism and the cash nexus enter the picture. Over the years, as the price of participation has increased enormously, the cause of transformation might not be a racial or cultural divide so much as it is a financial impossibility for some people to play *mas*. Similarly, the steel bands, traditionally associated with poor and working-class Blacks, have also acquired an economic dimension. For as costs increase, it is becoming increasingly impossible to sustain a steel band without corporate sponsorship. Thus, Lee (1991) questioned whether the steel band and the traditional *masque* would have suffered the same fate had they been products of the middle or elite classes. The diminishing statuses of forms long associated with Carnival are not the result of a dominant African presence, but rather of a takeover by the middle class (much of which is resident outside of the country), which has led to the commercialization and capitalization of Carnival festivities under the guise of a nationalist or pluralist agenda.

CONCLUSIONS

Carnival, with its race and class controversies, is the great mirror of Trinidadian society that has historically reflected its social divisions. It has been an arena in which struggles arising from these divisions have been enacted, or played out. Trinidad is a capitalist society where class divisions have coincided with those of race and color. Therefore, although race continues to be an important and sometimes overriding political factor, the tensions of Carnival arise more out of class than race divisions.

Thus, in the final analysis, Carnival remains a performance, whereby conflicting ideas and values are dramatized and contested in the struggle for power. It is a stage on which the complexities and contradictions of the nation are articulated. And despite many of its elements being historically controlled and manipulated by different classes to serve their own narrow interests, the Carnival voice of resistance has never been completely silenced. Indeed, Carnival today is still not the exclusive cultural property of the middle class, despite their best efforts to appropriate it. Because the character of Carnival remains ambiguous and contradictory, it cannot be owned. As a symbol of Trinidadian culture and society, Carnival's most powerful element is its ambiguity, which allows it to express ideals and their opposites simultaneously (Van Koningsbruggen, 1997). Carnival is not a single, monolithic, or unified thing; it is a multicomplexity of parallel practices with multiple meanings and therefore can satisfy a plethora of conflicting needs at the same time.

Carnival, then, is not an African but a Trinidadian tradition; one that serves to encapsulate the fluid, evolving, complex, and multiple political, social, and economic contexts that define not only the nation of Trinidad, but its people. What may have been started by African slaves in the French colonial context has now spread to encompass peoples, cultures, and traditions that are neither African, French, Roman Catholic, nor colonial. Carnival is not only about class and race divides and conflicts, but also about accommodation. And although some like Smart and Nehusi (2000) may dispute its racial origins and ownership, what cannot be disputed is that Carnival is about defining multiple cultures where being African (or Afro) or Indian (or Indo) is wholly a social invention.

REFERENCES

Adeyinka, O. N. (2000). A carnival of resistance, emancipation, commemoration, reconstruction, and creativity. In I. I. Smart & K. S. K. Nehusi (Eds.), *Ah come back home: Perspectives on the Trinidad and Tobago carnival* (pp. 105–129). Washington, DC: Original World Press.

Allahar, A. L. (1994). More than an oxymoron: The social construction of primordial attachment. *Canadian Ethnic Studies, 26*, 18–33.

Allahar, A. L. (1995). The making of Caribbean identities. *Transition, 24*, 27–51.

Allahar, A. L. (1996). Primordialism and ethnic political mobilization in modern society. *New Community, 22*, 5–22.

Allahar, A. L. (1998). Popular culture and racialisation of political consciousness in Trinidad and Tobago. *Wadadagei: A Journal of the Caribbean and Its Diaspora, 1*, 1–41.

Alleyne-Dettmers, P. (2000). Beyond borders, carnival as global phenomena: "Going bananas, food for the devil." In I. I. Smart & K. S. K. Nehusi (Eds.), *Ah come back home: Perspectives on the Trinidad and Tobago carnival* (pp. 131–162). Washington, DC: Original World Press.

Anthony, M. (1989). *Parade of the carnivals of Trinidad, 1839–1989.* Port of Spain, Trinidad: Circle.

Braithwaite, L., & Crichlow, M. (1991). Stratification, pluralism and economic power. In S. Ryan (Ed.), *Social and occupational stratification in contemporary Trinidad and Tobago* (pp. 52–58). Port of Spain, Trinidad: University of the West Indies Press.

Brereton, B. (1975). The Trinidad carnival 1870–1900. *Savacou, 11–12*, 46–57.

Burton, R. D. (1997). *Afro-Creole: Power, opposition and play in the Caribbean.* Ithaca, NY: Cornell University Press.

Cowley, J. (1996). *Carnival, canboulay and calypso traditions in the making.* Cambridge, England: Cambridge University Press.

De Freitas, P. A. (1994). *Playing mas: The construction and deconstruction of national identity in the Trinidad carnival*. Unpublished doctoral dissertation, MacMaster University, Hamilton, Ontario, Canada.
Deosaran, R. (1981). Some issues in multiculturalism: The case of Trinidad and Tobago in a post-colonial era. *Ethnic Groups, 3*, 199–225.
Eriksen, T. H. (1992). Multiple traditions and the question of cultural integration. *Ethnos, 57,* 5–30.
Greene, E. (1974). *Race vs. politics in Guyana.* Port of Spain, Trinidad: Institute of Social and Economic Research, University of the West Indies Press.
Halapua, W. (2001). *The role of militarism in the politics of Fiji.* Unpublished doctoral dissertation, University of the South Pacific, Suva, Fiji.
Hill, D. R. (1993). *Calypso calaloo: Early carnival music in Trinidad.* Gainesville: University Press of Florida.
Hill, E. (1972). *The Trinidad carnival: Mandate for national theatre.* Austin: Texas University Press.
Hill, E. (1985). Traditional figures in Carnival: Their preservation, development, and interpretation. *Caribbean Quarterly, 31*(2), 14–34.
Ho, C. G. T. (2000). Popular culture and the aestheticization of politics: Hegemonic struggle and postcolonial nationalism in the Trinidad carnival. *Transforming Anthropology, 9,* 3–18.
Jha, J. (1974). The Indian heritage in Trinidad. In J. La Guerre (Ed.), *Calcutta to Caroni* (pp. 1–25). London: Longman.
Johnson, K. (1984). The social impact of carnival. In Institute of Social and Economic Studies (Ed.), *The social and economic impact of carnival*, (pp. 173–207). Mona, Jamaica: University of the West Indies Press.
Lee, A. (1991). Class, race, color, and the Trinidad carnival. In S. Ryan (Ed.), *Social and occupational stratification in contemporary Trinidad and Tobago* (pp. 417–433). Port of Spain, Trinidad: University of the West Indies Press.
Malik, Y. (1971). *East Indians in Trinidad.* New York: Oxford University Press.
Martin, V. (2000). Coming back home to take home back. In I. I. Smart & K. S. K. Nehusi (Eds.), *Ah come back home: Perspectives on the Trinidad and Tobago carnival* (pp. 179–195). Washington, DC: Original World Press.
Mason, P. (1998). *Bacchanal! The carnival culture of Trinidad.* Philadelphia: Temple University Press.
Miller, D. (1991). Absolute freedom in Trinidad. *Man, 26,* 323–341.
Mintz, S. W. (1981). The Caribbean region. In R. Marx-Delson (Ed.), *Readings in Caribbean history and economics* (pp. 6–12). London: Gordon & Breach.
Moran, P. (2000). Experiencing the pan-African dimension of carnival. In I. I. Smart & K. S. K. Nehusi (Eds.), *Ah come back home: Perspectives on the Trinidad and Tobago carnival* (pp. 163–177). Washington, DC: Original World Press.
Nehusi, K. S. K. (2000a). Going back home to the carnival. In I. I. Smart & K. S. K. Nehusi (Eds.), *Ah come back home: Perspectives on the Trinidad and Tobago carnival* (pp. 1–16). Washington, DC: Original World Press.
Nehusi, K. S. K. (2000b). The origins of carnival: Notes from a preliminary investigation. In I. I. Smart & K. S. K. Nehusi (Eds.), *Ah come back home: Perspectives on the Trinidad and Tobago carnival* (pp. 77–103). Washington, DC: Original World Press.
Puri, S. (1997). Race, rape, and representation: Indo-Caribbean women and cultural nationalism. *Cultural Critiques, 14,* 119–163.
Reddock, R. (1999). Jahaji bhai: The emergence of a dougla poetics in Trinidad and Tobago. *Identities, 5,* 569–601.
Rohlehr, G. (1990). *Calypso and society in pre-independence Trinidad.* Port of Spain, Trinidad: Author.
Ryan, S. (1991). *Social and occupational stratification in contemporary Trinidad and Tobago.* Port of Spain, Trinidad: University of the West Indies Press.
Samaroo, B. (1987). Two abolitions: African slavery and East Indian indentureship. In D. Dabydeen & B. Samaroo (Eds.), *India in the Caribbean* (pp. 25–41). London: University of Warwick.

Scott, J. C. (1990). *Domination and the arts of resistance: Hidden transcripts.* New Haven, CT: Yale University Press.
Singh, K. (1974). East Indians in larger society. In J. La Guerre (Ed.), *Calcutta to Caroni: The East Indians of Trinidad* (pp. 39–58). London: Longman.
Smart, I. I. (2000a). Carnival, the ultimate pan-African festival. In I. I. Smart & K. S. K. Nehusi (Eds.), *Ah come back home: Perspectives on the Trinidad and Tobago carnival* (pp. 29–76). Washington, DC: Original World Press.
Smart, I. I. (2000b). It's not French (Europe), it's really French-based Creole (Africa). In I. I. Smart & K. S. K. Nehusi (Eds.), *Ah come back home: Perspectives on the Trinidad and Tobago carnival* (pp. 197–221). Washington, DC: Original World Press.
Smart, I. I., & Nehusi, K. S. K. (Eds.). (2000). *Ah come back home: Perspectives on the Trinidad and Tobago carnival.* Washington, DC: Original World Press.
Springer, P. E. (2000). Carnival: Identity, ethnicity and spirituality. In I. I. Smart & K. S. K. Nehusi (Eds.), *Ah come back home: Perspectives on the Trinidad and Tobago carnival* (pp. 17–27). Washington, DC: Original World Press.
Stuempfle, S. (1995). *The steelband movement: The forging of national art in Trinidad and Tobago.* Mona, Jamaica: University of the West Indies Press.
Traube, E. (1996). The popular in American culture. *Annual Review of Anthropology, 25,* 127–151.
Trotman, D. V. (1991). The image of calypso: Trinidad 1946–1986. In S. Ryan (Ed.), *Social and occupational stratification in contemporary Trinidad and Tobago* (pp. 385–398). St. Augustine, Trinidad: University of the West Indies Press.
Van Koningsbruggen, P. (1997). *Trinidad carnival: A quest for national identity.* London: Macmillan.
Williams, E. (1960). Race relations in the Caribbean. In V. Rubin (Ed.), *Caribbean studies: A symposium* (2nd ed., pp. 54–60). Seattle: University of Washington Press.
Williams, E. (1962). *History of people in Trinidad and Tobago.* Port of Spain, Trinidad: PNM.
Yelvington, K. (1993). *Trinidad ethnicity.* London: Macmillan.

Pariah Status, Identity, and Creativity in Babylon: Utopian Visions of Home in the African Diaspora

Janet L. DeCosmo
Center for Caribbean Culture, Humanities
Florida A & M University

In this article I explore the complex relationships among diasporic identity, home, and marginality in the context of Rastafari philosophy and practice. Groups within the African diaspora believe that globalization and the "We are all one" slogan exist to create one huge market for the benefit of the multinational and international corporate elites. Not only has the Black underclass in the diaspora continued to expand rather than shrink, but, in many ways, Blacks are further behind Whites than they have been in the past. In an effort to survive with some modicum of dignity and self-respect, they have attempted to counter the trend toward global neoapartheid. Rastafari have intentionally chosen to identify themselves not only as Blacks (the children of Africa), but as "marginals" outside of the domain of Babylon. They take pride in the fact that they have rejected the values of the new world order.

In this article I will demonstrate the relevance to African diaspora discourse of the concepts of "pariah status" and "homelessness" employed by Max Weber and Hannah Arendt in their analyses of Jewish and Christian diasporic populations. The term *pariah* was used by Weber in the early 1920s to describe ancient Judaism and early Christianity, religions whose purpose was to provide explanations for the suffering and loss of dignity experienced by ethnically marginalized groups displaced from their homeland. Because their status was not positively valued, Weber maintained, these groups nourished their sense of dignity by identifying themselves as specially chosen by God to fulfill the conditions by which a return

---

Requests for reprints should be sent to Janet L. DeCosmo, Director, Center for Caribbean Culture, Humanities, Florida A & M University, Tallahassee, FL 32307. E-mail: janet.decosmo@famu.edu

home could be effected (Weber, 1922/1964). The ethical imperative became that of breaking with the established institutionalized order, symbolized by Babylon.

Arendt applied the term *pariah* extensively in her analysis of diasporic Jews whom she defined as homeless (or worldless). For her the rootlessness of the "wandering Jew" antedated the rootlessness of many in the modern age. The lack of what she called a "privately owned share of a common world" (1978, p. 99) had been a condition of the Jews' existence since the beginning of the Diaspora. She agreed with Weber that this condition of worldlessness or world alienation often led to the development of new forms of religion as well as vital new expressions in art, poetry, and music. In her study of 17th century Jewish mysticism, Arendt (1978) wrote:

> Today, as in the past, [mystical] speculations appeal to all who are actually excluded from action, prevented from altering a fate that appears to them unbearable and, feeling themselves helpless victims of incomprehensible forces, are naturally inclined to find some secret means for gaining power for participating in the "drama of the World." (p. 99)

The important question for both Arendt and Weber was whether diasporic populations would go on to create or join a political community that would protect their dignity and rights. *Home* for both these thinkers meant territory or land and the power to defend it. For them, there was no such thing as human dignity or rights without a political community to protect those rights. Weber (1946) defined the state as that "human community that (successfully) claims the monopoly of the legitimate use of force within a given territory" (p. 78). If the state refuses to protect the rights and dignity of marginal or pariah groups or even actively begins to take them away, genocide may be the ultimate result. Thus, in a world with no impartial third party with the power to uphold international laws regarding human dignity and rights, groups cannot afford to be stateless or worldless; without power there can be no rights or dignity.

Neither Weber nor Arendt would be surprised by what has come to be called the "new world order." The transformation of global society, or globalization, entails the unfortunate triumph of global "democracy"/consumerism based on the U.S. corporate hegemonic model. Indeed, as Berman (2000) pointed out, "of the world's one hundred largest economies, 51 are corporations rather than countries, and 70% of world trade is engaged in by the 500 largest corporations" (p. 63). Weber predicted the future would become an "iron cage" created by the global spread of a functionally rational, bureaucratic capitalism, and Arendt pointed both to the "banality of evil" as well as to tendencies toward totalitarianism in the modern world. Both agreed with Marx that surplus populations would increase and that there would be a growing social and economic inequality, not only within nations but between the core and periphery nations of the world as well. However, they did not live long enough to see what has become the new religion of corporate consumerism and the resultant spiritual anomie that pervades the planet as it is being turned into a giant shopping mall.

THE GLOBAL SOUL

There is a new postmodern identity to go along with the new globalism: the "global soul," or "nowhereian." According to Iyer (2000), who considers himself to be a global soul, such a person has no identity or can continually reinvent his or her identity. Such a person has

> grown up in many cultures all at once—and so lived in the cracks between them—or might be one who, though rooted in background, lived and worked on a globe that propelled him from tropics to snowstorm in three hours. She might have a name that gave away nothing about her nationality (a name like Kim, say, or Maya, or Tara), and she might have a porous sense of self that changed with her location. Even the most ageless human rites—scattering his father's ashes, or meeting the woman who might be his wife—he might find himself performing six thousand miles from the place he now called home. (pp. 18–19)

Although the nowhereian has global mobility, he or she has no sense of fixed community or home. The nowhereian is a person who falls between all the categories and whose boundaries are blurred. Although Iyer (2000) saw this condition, at least partly, he wistfully wrote that "the very notion of home is foreign to me, as the state of foreignness is the closest thing I know to home" (p. 24).

To his credit, Iyer (2000) realized that those growing up simultaneously in two or three different cultures are still a tiny minority, and a relatively comfortable one. As he admitted,

> the most urgent issues in the world today ... are still the ones they've always been: how to get food on the table, and find shelter for your children; how to live beyond tomorrow. Indeed, one of the most troubling features of the globalism we celebrate is that the so-called linking of the planet has, in fact, intensified the distance between people: the richest 358 people in the world, by U.N. calculations, have a financial worth as great as that of 2.3 billion others. (p. 24)

THE AFRICAN DIASPORA

Groups within the African diaspora are well aware that globalization and the "We are all one" slogan exists to create one huge market and line the pockets of the multinational and international corporate elites. Not only has the Black underclass in the diaspora continued to expand rather than shrink, but, in many ways, Blacks are further behind Whites than they have been in the past. In an effort to survive with some modicum of dignity and self-respect, they have attempted to counter the trend toward global neoapartheid. They have intentionally chosen to identify themselves not only as Blacks (the children of Africa), but as "marginals" outside of the domain of Babylon. They take pride in the fact that they have rejected the values of the new world order.

For example, a Rastafari[1] ghetto dweller in Bahia, Brazil, who wears dreadlocks and whose arms are covered with tattoos, told me:

> These tattoos are a letter, the name of this letter is "words of wisdom." With this letter what happens? People will not relate to me by the color of my skin; they deal with me because of intelligence, because of love ... I'm a mural because on my body I go back to the roots of the African people, of the less fortunate poor ones. But even the very small can give a rich spiritual presence.

This individual vigorously condemned the capitalist system:

> I do not believe in capitalism. Capitalism was taken away from my life. To maintain this hair, I cannot invest in the system. Not a cent. I live from the powers, like Daniel, like Joshua. I live like Jesus Christ. I live spirit because I am spirit. If I live in spirit, I have to walk in spirit. People do not understand why I do not need money to live. I do not need government. I live theocracy.

Interestingly, this commentator believed that one day the tables would be turned and the powerless would take power. He said

> When we get the chance to get in the government, in power, we're going to start a new program, planting and sharing and dividing. We are all partners on the land. Why didn't we have participation in Brazilian oil and gold? We are a people of the planet. Why aren't the universal riches of the world invested in us? We have to do that. When we ascend, we have to give people what they deserve: dignity. What I understand by dignity is that man is an instrument of love, to love. Love your neighbor like you love yourself. ... Fraternity. To give up, extinguish, and banish away capitalism from the earth. No money. Culture of Jah, yes. Amen.

This individual believed that he was a chosen instrument of *Jah*, a tool to fight against Babylon. This view, common to Rastafaris the world over, may be traced to Garvey, who asserted that Blacks were the chosen people created in the image of God—a Black God—and that Africa was the promised land. Garvey explained:

> Up to now we have found no race in power that has held out a helping hand and protection to all humanity, and it is apparent that that position is left for the new Ethiopia. ... We shall be the elect of God. He must have had His purpose when He took us through

---

[1] Since the terms *Rastafarianism* and *Rastafarians* have been rejected by its adherents, the term *Rastafari* is used herein to refer to the ideology/religion/way of life itself, as well as to an individual or a group of proponents.

the rigors of slavery for more than two hundred and fifty years ... and I attribute it to that prophecy of God that His children shall one day stretch forth their hands again unto Him. (as cited in Burkett, 1978, p. 56)

Garvey's political and economic programs were expressed in religious vocabulary, and religious grounding in scripture provided justification for his goals. Yet the religious themes were set into an uncompromisingly this-worldly context. As one preacher explained, "The black man, if he ever expects to become what the U.N.I.A. is striving to make him, must learn to fight. ... If you do not have a bit of heaven here, don't worry, you won't have any hereafter" (as cited in Burkett, 1978, p. 130).

Garvey's passionate demand for social justice meant a fair distribution of power in *this* world, not a spiritual reward in the next. And the redemption of Africa—"a national home of our own"—meant achieving self-sufficiency and worldly power. These beliefs were then transmitted from the Garveyites to the early Rastafaris in Jamaica, and then to reggae musicians and poets such as Bob Marley, whose music, in turn, has helped create a new global Rastafari identity.

RASTAFARIS AND DIASPORA

Rastafaris have continued to resist Babylon and the new world order by inverting its values: They choose to live modestly rather than emulate society's elite consumers. They have scorned the corporate/commercial way of life. Democratic discussions, or "reasonings," in Rastafari yards allow them to debate the merits of various ideas and ideologies and to freely interpret a wide variety of reading materials. Schools and universities, they maintain, exist for the purpose of miseducation. As Bob Marley (1976) sang in "Crazy Baldhead" (from *Rastaman Vibration*), "I and I build the cabin, I and I plant the corn, didn't my people before me slave for this country? ... We build your penitentiaries, we build your schools, brainwash education, to make us the fools." And, as Pulis (1999) noted, it is not just the content of Rastafari teaching that is counter-hegemonic, but the reasoning itself: "The very process whereby the Rastafari world view is constructed in an ongoing and dynamic way ... subverts the dominant print-based culture" (p. 186).

As a further development of Garveyism, the Rastafari way of life can best be seen as a response not only to racial and class oppression but to the homelessness, rootlessness, and dehumanization that such oppression has engendered. Like Garvey himself, who had been a migrant laborer in Panama, Rastafaris came to perceive themselves as doubly homeless as they increasingly left the Caribbean for better prospects elsewhere. As Campbell (1987) wrote, "[T]wice removed from their homeland in Africa and from their adopted home in the Caribbean, the Rastafari, as part of the black population of Europe, yearned for a land which they could call their home" (p. 8). Laments about the condition of homelessness can frequently be heard in the lyrics of reggae. As Bob Andy sang:

This couldn't be my home,
It must be somewhere else,
Can't get no clothes to wear,
Can't get no food to eat,
Can't get a job to get bread,
That's why I've got to go back home. (As cited in Campbell, 1987, p. 135)

Even those Rastafaris who remained in the Caribbean experienced what Arendt described as worldlessness: Although technically they were citizens, their "second-class" status did not allow for them to become a functioning part of the political community. There was thus the perception that no political community existed that would guarantee their dignity and rights. As Walter Rodney stated, "Our history has been bedevilled by the fact that we, as a colonized people in the Western world, have never had a power to which we could turn, and that our oppressors have never felt any sense of having to account to somebody else for the treatment which they accorded us" (as cited in Cambpell, 1987, p. 220).

THE PARIAH STATUS OF RASTAFARIS

As was the case with the Garveyites, a return to the original homeland of Africa became the focus of Jamaican Rastafaris. They pointed to Garvey's statement that:

> Every race must find a home; hence ... [Blacks] are raising the cry of "Africa for the Africans," those at home and those abroad ... the thoughtful and industrious of our race want to go back to Africa, because we realize it will be our only hope of permanent existence. (as cited in Tafari, 1985, pp. 9–10)

To create a new identity and a new sense of self-respect, they employed what Arendt called a typical pariah strategy. They used elements of their cultural inheritance that were of great antiquity. Like the ancient Hebrews had done before them, they claimed to be God's chosen people and projected their powerlessness into an ultimate future power outside the oppression of Babylon. An example can be found in one of Bob Marley's songs that asserts, "We are the children of the Rasta Man—we are the children of the Higher Man" (Marley, 1979). Another of his songs contends, "Some are leaves, some are branches, but I and I are the roots" (Marley, 1986).

Even in the formative years of Rastafari, when the Jamaican state actively harassed dreadlocked sufferers, the pariah strategy worked: People who might have disintegrated into an undisciplined mob with no morality were able to maintain their self-respect and their family and community ties. The idea that they were part of a higher reality caused them to try to act in accordance with this higher reality, thus becoming an instrument whereby they could actively participate in the destiny of humankind. Thus Rastafari became a form of cultural resistance.

Historically, in the quest to overcome a politically immobilizing colonial mentality, appeals to identity are vital. As Barnet and Muller (1974) wrote:

> A crucial organizational strategy for those societies which have made real steps toward solving the problems of mass misery, unemployment, and inequality, has been to mobilize the population by encouraging their sense of identity, as individuals and as members of a national community. A succession of visitors to China, Cuba, Tanzania, and North Vietnam have been struck by the genuine enthusiasm of the people to participate in what they are repeatedly told are great social experiments. In these countries the population is continually being asked to believe that they are "new people" who by virtue of their own abilities and energies are able to transform their societies in ways unknown in human history. Backed by the power of the state, the primary appeal is to personal and national pride. (p. 178)

Rastafari has become a transnational, or global, form of resistance. Nevertheless, there is a strong holistic philosophy or feeling of unity or "oneness" in Rastafaris, no matter where they find themselves in the world. This sense of oneness is evidenced in the very language they use; for example, the use of the plural "I and I" rather than the singular "I." Nichols (1979) explained:

> "I" is so important that a Rasta will never say "I went home," but would say instead "I and I went home," to include the presence and divinity of the Almighty with himself every time he speaks. "I and I" also includes bredren, who also say "I and I." In this simple way, through language, Rastafari is a community of people all the time. (p. 38)

Rastafari identity is thus being shaped beyond national borders.

An important component of early Rastafari in Jamaica inherited from the Garveyites was the idea of repatriation to Africa. However, this emphasis is not present everywhere in all the diaspora. Although all of the Rastafari informants I spoke with in Salvador, Bahia (Brazil), consider their heritage to be African Brazilian or African, none of them spoke of moving to Africa permanently. Unlike the first generation of Rastafaris in Jamaica, none expressed belief in a massive exodus to Africa brought about by either divine or human agency. One informant expressed the view that they were already there in spirit. He said: "If Jesus leads me to go to Jamaica [or Africa], yes [I would go]. To want and to do something comes from Jah. If it is his desire, I will come to all these places. But we know that spiritually we are in all these places."

Some of the Bahian Rastafari informants expressed dismay at their lack of political organization. They are in a state of disagreement about the potential of Rastafaris to effect political change directly. They nevertheless describe themselves as fighters and revolutionaries. A predominant theme in reggae music is the prophetic command to challenge the system and demand justice. The Wailers insisted in "Get Up, Stand Up" (on the album *Burnin'*) that sufferers "stand up for your rights" and "don't give up the fight" because "life is your right" (Marley, 1973). According to

Owens (1976), the term *revolution* for Rastafaris meant something different than a violent coup or a toppling of the system; it meant "a change of heart and mind, such as indicated by the cultivation of locks" (p. 208). As one Rastafari told him, "When you wear the locks, you are a revolutionist" (p. 208).

Lindsay (in press) explained that for Rastafaris, the revolutionary process is one of "psychocultural demystification; it is everyday resistance to oppression, not something imposed from above by vanguard elites." In their effort to reeducate the masses, Rastafaris provide the cultural counter-symbols whereby the system itself can be challenged and eventually transformed. Thus, there is virtually no disagreement about the importance of Rastafarian cultural contributions that help educate people and change their consciousness.

Ironically, a large part of the reason for the successful spread of Rastafari culture may have been their original marginal or pariah status. Again, Arendt's insights were prescient. In her analysis of the situation of the Jews in Europe after the Enlightenment and emancipation, she distinguished between *conscious pariahs* and *parvenus*. Parvenus were those Jews who tried to succeed in the world of the Gentiles by seeking to escape their own community. Conscious pariahs did not, and as a result were often marginalized, even in relation to their own community. However, conscious pariahs creatively denied the social order by confronting it with a higher reality, which found expression in art, poetry, and music. Nettleford (1989), too, realized that the creative energies of his people came not from an upper class elite but from the bottom. About Caribbean arts, he wrote: "A great many, if not most, of the artists in these fields have been drawn largely from the unlettered commonfold—the people from below who are traditionally marginalized and denigrated" (p. 245). They intentionally wore dreadlocks, beards, and colors that would mark their identity as conscious pariahs (their music, coincidentally, is known as *conscious reggae*).

Seemingly aware of Marxian sensibilities, Rastafaris are deeply concerned with the violence being done to the sufferers by the system. That is, even in an absence of armed conflict, when political and economic systems cause great oppression and suffering, a type of institutional violence is being perpetrated against a powerless people. As death-of-God theologian Rubenstein (1975) argued: "It is absurd to pretend that government has a responsibility to protect its citizens from theft and physical assault but has no responsibility to defend them from the infinitely greater violence perpetrated, often mindlessly, by institutions and policies that render millions of human beings literally useless" (p. 96). Rastafaris insist that each person has a right to a place of dignity and social utility within the community.

Rastafari might also be seen as a type of folk community, or folk culture. As opposed to mass culture or the culture of globalization, where ties between group members are rational, nonemotional, and contractual, the ties in ethnic or folk culture are emotionally determined, giving group members a sense of mutual involvement. However, as Rubenstein (1966) reminded us: "Each social arrangement has its advantages and disadvantages. However, lest the importance of folk-culture be overestimated, the importance in super-culture [mass culture] of privacy, mobility, and anonymity for personal growth must not be forgotten" (p. 23). Nevertheless, this writer would suggest that there is something to be gained from identifying oneself as a Rastafari and by positing a mythical Africa as home.

CONCLUSIONS: AFRICA AND THE MYTH OF HOME

African diaspora scholars have pointed out the dangers of essentialism and how difficult it is to draw a line between what is truly African and what is not. Mythical or not, however, "memories" of Africa and a sense of roots have served those who dwell in the diaspora well. Ancestral mores were held on to as a psychological necessity. As Okpewho, Davies, and Mazrui (1999) wrote of African Americans:

> Long after emancipation, and during reconstruction, the old sense of roots continued to express itself even when time had steadily taken a toll on memories of Africa. ... Africa remained in the subconscious as some kind of psychological surety, to be invoked against a system and a culture they revolted intensely against. (p. xv)

The idea of Africa as home is part of the collective psyche of groups such as Rastafaris within the African diaspora. It aids in resisting systems of oppression under which they have been forced to live in the new world order. Although as a scholar I find it objectionable when African myth is taught as history, I am sympathetic to the opportunistic use of the Africa-as-home idea when it offers those on the bottom a way to cope or to survive in intact communities and overcome the hardship and distress that come with being treated as largely superfluous. The reason I am sympathetic is that the idea of the "upward march of civilization" is a myth. As Rubenstein (1975) wrote:

> Civilization means slavery, wars, exploitation, and death camps. It also means medical hygiene, elevated religious ideals, beautiful art, and exquisite music. It is an error to imagine that civilization and savage cruelty are antitheses. On the contrary, in every organic process, the antitheses always reflect a unified totality, and civilization is an organic process. Mankind never emerged out of savagery into civilization. ... In our times the cruelties ... have become far more effectively administered than ever before. They have not and will not cease to exist. (p. 92)

Given that the 20th century was a century of bureaucratic violence and mass death, then any ideology or philosophy that uplifts a people is justified. Two questions that must be raised, however, are the following: Can the African diaspora (or segments of it) play a role in international politics through "traveling cultures" such as Rastafari and thus become a vehicle for international action and development? And secondly, if Rastafari identity is a global one, can their dignity and rights be protected outside of national borders?

REFERENCES

Arendt, H. (1978). *The Jew as pariah: Jewish identity and politics in the modern age.* New York: Grove.
Barrett, L. E. (1988). *The Rastafarians: Sounds of cultural dissonance.* Boston: Beacon.
Berman, M. (2000). *The twilight of American culture.* New York: Norton.
Burkett, R. K. (1978). *Garveyism as a religious movement.* Metuchen, NJ: Scarecrow.
Campbell, H. (1987). *Rasta and resistance: From Marcus Garvey to Walter Rodney.* Trenton, NJ: Africa World Press.
Iyer, P. (2000). *The global soul: Jet lag, shopping malls, and the search for home.* New York: Knopf.
Lindsay, L. (in press). Beating down Babylon: Marley and the politics of subversion. In *Marley's music: Reggae, Rastafari, and Jamaican culture.* Kingston, Jamaica: University of the West Indies Press.
Marley, B. (1973) Get up, stand up. On *Burnin'* [CD], London: Island Records.
Marley, B. (1976) *Rastaman Vibration* [CD], London: Island Records.
Marley, B. (1979). Africa unite. On *Survival* [CD], London: Island Records.
Marley, B. (1986). Roots. On *Rebel music* [CD], London: Island Records.
Nettleford, R. (1989). Cultural identity and the arts—New horizons for the Caribbean social sciences? *Social and Economic Studies, 38,* 235–263.
Nichols, T. (1979). *Rastafari: A way of life.* Garden City, NY: Anchor.
Okpewho, I., Davies, C. B., & Mazrui, A. A. (1999). *The African diaspora: African origins and new world identities.* Bloomington: Indiana University Press.
Owens, J. (1976). *Dread: The Rastafarians of Jamaica.* Kingston, Jamaica: Sangster's Book.
Pulis, J. W. (1999). *Religion, diaspora, and cultural identity: A reader in the Anglophone Caribbean.* Garden City, NY: Gordon & Breach.
Rubenstein, R. L. (1966). *After Auschwitz: Radical theology and contemporary Judaism.* Indianapolis, IN: Bobbs-Merrill.
Rubenstein, R. L. (1975). *The cunning of history: Mass death and the American future.* New York: Harper & Row.
Tafari, J. I. (1985). The Rastafari—Successors of Marcus Garvey. *Caribbean Quarterly, 26*(4), 9–10.
Weber, M. (1946). Politics as a vocation. In H. H. Gerth & C. Wright Mills (Trans. and Eds.), *From Max Weber: Essays in sociology* (pp. 77–128). New York: Oxford University Press.
Weber, M. (1964). *The sociology of religion.* Boston: Beacon. (Original work published 1922)
Weber, M. (1976). The social psychology of the world religions. In H. H. Gerth and C. Wright Mills, *From Max Weber: Essays in sociology* (pp. 267–301). New York: Oxford University Press. (Original work published 1922/23)

Colón Man Version: Oppositional Narratives and Jamaican Identity in Michael Thelwell's *The Harder They Come*

Rhonda D. Frederick
Department of English
Boston College

Mainstream histories portray Colón Men, workers named after Panamá's Caribbean port city, as inexpensive labor. Such approaches, therefore, offer little insight into why these laborers are honored in Caribbean literature and culture. It stands to reason that other stories inform Colón Men's literary incarnations. Imagined and imaginable truths—available in oppositional narratives of Panamá Canal migrants—convey realities that are not available in traditional versions of this history. As a result, such truths allow readers to interpret the character of Nathaniel Francis in Michael Thelwell's *The Harder They Come*. This essay argues that Thelwell uses creative and oppositional Panamá narratives to fashion his canal worker. It then posits that the author employs the Colón Man to shape protagonist "Rhygin" Martin into a revolutionary Jamaican subject. Both in the character of Nathaniel (made out of fact and imagination) and through his narrative interests, Thelwell offers his version of a uniquely Afro-Jamaican identity.

> [Nattie] had been to Panama and had made a lot of money digging a canal. Ivan wasn't sure what that was, but all the white men that came to dig it got sick and died, so they had to send for black men. An' Maas' Nattie had gone and had not died ... But Maas' Nattie had become a foreman, an' did the job and come back with plenty money which he used to buy up plenty land.
>
> —Michael Thelwell,
> *The Harder They Come* (p. 38)

Requests for reprints should be sent to Rhonda D. Frederick, Department of English, Boston College, Chestnut Hill, MA 02467–3806. E-mail: frederir@bc.edu

If, as Christian (1987) argued, "literature is not an occasion for discourse among critics but is necessary nourishment for [the writer's] people and one way by which [these people] come to understand their lives better" (p. 53), then the task of better representing Caribbean subjectivity has important and practical implications. Speaking explicitly about the Caribbean, Glissant (1989) furthered Christian's assertion. For Glissant, Caribbean intellectuals were

> capable of carrying forward [their] people to self-renewal and of providing them with renewed ambition, by making them possess their world and their lived experience (wherein a Caribbean identity is present) and by making them fall into step with those who also share the same space. (pp. 223–224)

Caribbean writers/intellectuals contribute the region's alternative truths to proclaim a broader reality, one more representative of and useful to the people of the region. These scholars communicate an intricate view of their communities and reflect that view back onto its source. In seeing themselves, members of these communities experience a transformation of consciousness, toward Caribbeanness and away from a learned history of dependence.

If, as Lamming (1983) asserted, "at a deeper level of intention than literal accuracy, [the novelist] seeks to construct a world that might have been; to show the possible as a felt and living reality" (p. xiv), then Michael Thelwell, author of *The Harder They Come* (1988), was engaged in something larger than creative expression. He wrote another reality, but wrote it *into* prevailing discourses of victimization and dependence. His articulation of an oppositional Jamaican subjectivity intended to transform the consciousness of Jamaica's rural and working class populations and to complicate predetermined notions about them and their country. He used his characters, Colon Man Nathaniel Francis and protagonist Ivanhoe "Rhygin" Martin, to write/right a story that often only recognized the United States' influence on this Caribbean country. His work declared, as Glissant (1989) suitably stated, that "our Caribbean reality is an option open to us. It springs from our natural experience, but in our histories has only been [seen as] 'an ability to survive'" (p. 22). In assisting Jamaican readers toward a better understanding of their lives, Thelwell tried to reflect onto such readers the strength derived from envisioning themselves as more than "colonized" and interpreting their hisories and stories as more than "responses to colonialism." To state this another way, I find that Thelwell advanced a notion of Caribbeanness as a complex subjectivity evolving from complex circumstances.

THE COLÓN MAN IN HISTORIES AND STORIES

The Colón Man, named after Panamá's Caribbean port city, was born out of his emigration to as well as his work on the isthmian railroad and canal. He could be identified by his cocky attitude, money and clothes, broadened worldview, masculinity, and even by his illnesses. Largely because of the cultural and social significance of these features, Colón Men have come to signify two important events in the Caribbean: one of its largest internal migrations and the construction of the Panamá Canal.

Yet mainstream histories portray Colón Men, when they include them at all, merely as available and inexpensive labor. Such characterizations are all the more demeaning when one considers that canal authorities counted Caribbean workers as "freight, very expensive freight" (McCullough, 1977, p. 111). Traditional approaches to canal history, therefore, offer little insight into why these laborers hold an honored place in Caribbean literature and culture. It then stands to reason that other stories inform Colón Man's literary and cultural incarnations. Imagined and imaginable truths—available in creative and oppositional narratives about Panamá migrants—convey realities that are apparently unavailable in traditional versions of this history. Thus, it is through imaginative perspectives on Colón Men that readers can understand the significance of Master Nathaniel Francis (Maas' Nattie) in *The Harder They Come*.

In *New World Adams: Conversations With Contemporary West Indian Writers*, Thelwell described himself as a political activist who writes (as cited in Dance, 1992, p. 252). Thus he used his novel to support particular politics in Jamaica. He wrote the novel after being approached by a representative from Grove Press who thought Perry Henzell's film *The Harder They Come* (Henzell, 1973) "had in it the basis for a very good book about Third World experience" (Dance, 1992, p. 246). Although Thelwell secured a publisher before he wrote his novel (which suggests that Grove Press determined the novel's intention), he had prior plans about what he wanted this novel to do:

> the realities of Jamaican society and culture were being discussed in a much more accurate, a much more meaningful and productive kind of way, and I wanted to make a contribution to that. What I didn't think was that any white publisher in [the United States] would be interested in the kind of book that could do that, so that when Grove Press came up with this idea it struck me that here was precisely the vehicle I was looking for ... so I thought that since here was a publisher interested in this project it would give me a chance to write a novel about the peasants and the workers in Jamaica, about their culture, about their view of the world. (as cited in Dance, 1992, pp. 246–247)

Thus the novel was born. The publisher wanted a novel that gave a Western audience a detailed look at the exotic. Because the film was set in Jamaica and used Jamaican dialect (so much so that "English" subtitles were added), *The Harder They Come* was decidedly a foreign film. But because Jamaica was largely familiar in a specific (tourist) context, the film was "known" mainly through this limited purview. For a Western audience, then, the film was a complicated mix of the familiar (a tourist's Jamaica) and the unfamiliar (the language and an islander's reality). It is therefore understandable that Western viewers did not immediately register the film's revolutionary content. It is also understandable that the film's ambiguity and revolutionary theme are precisely what attracted Thelwell.

The author invests his novel with the ambiguity and rebellion inherent in the film by creating a family history for the celluloid protagonist. Revolutionary and complex features, as well as characteristics of other literary Colón Men, animate Nattie's character. Through the influence of this version of the Colón Man, Thelwell shapes the novel's Ivanhoe "Rhygin" Martin into a radical Jamaican subject. In fashioning the Colón Man character, the author mirrors processes through which Colón Men move through mainstream histories, oppositional stories, and imagined/imainable narratives about Panamá migrants. Nattie and his fictive and oppositional counterparts reject the prison in which mainstream history locks them. Thelwell extends this revisionary process to develop Ivan/Rhygin into a model of a uniquely Afro-Jamaican identity. The novel then projects Rhygin into an urban Jamaican landscape where he gives concrete form to struggles against poverty, classism, and United States' cultural hegemony.

MIGRATION HISTORIES AND PANAMA STORIES

One can argue that migration, forced and voluntary, is familiar to the Caribbean. When considering the large-scale movement of Europeans, Africans, and South Asians into the region, it appears that migration is almost as old as the Caribbean itself. It is therefore not surprising that representations of migrants and migrations recur in 19th- and 20th-century Caribbean literature. In his preface to *Return Migration and Remittances*, Bryce-Laporte (1982) stated that "epics on return immigrants are part of the lore and literature of many of the Caribbean islands; excellence, sometimes excesses, in leadership among repatriated statesmen and politicians have characterized much of contemporary Caribbean history" (p. xxv). If this idea holds generally for migration in the region, its implications for labor migration to the Panamanian isthmus are particularly remarkable. Lewis (1980) claimed that "almost every community in the West Indies had its own men who had gone to Panamá ... and had come back with savings enough to set them up for life" (p. 34). Possibly hyperbolic, Lewis's claim suggests the tremendous size of this movement. Recruited to work on the U.S.-backed Panamá Railroad (1850–1855), the canal venture initiated by French financier Ferdinand de Lesseps (1881–1898), and on the successfully completed U.S. canal (1904–1914), Caribbean men made isthmian labor migration the largest in the circum-Caribbean region.[1] The import of these mi-

---

[1] Investors from the United States backed the construction of the Panamá Railroad, intended to facilitate passage from the eastern United States to the newly discovered gold mines of California. Two French companies, the *Compagnie Universelle du Canal Interoceanique* and the *Compagnie Nouvelle du Canal de Panama*, attempted to build a transisthmian canal in Panamá from 1881–1894. Purchasing equipment and construction rights from the last French canal company, the U.S. Isthmian Canal Commission began building the Panamá Canal in 1904.

grations can be seen in the ways Caribbean creative writers depict Colón Men, illustrations shaped not only by mainstream history but also by oppositional and creative stories.

Mainstream or traditional approaches to the history of Panamá Canal construction customarily focus on issues concerning the United States or describe the project in terms of its engineering innovations. These kinds of historical accounts either fail to mention the army of Caribbean workers involved in its construction (Pepperman's *Who Built the Panama Canal?*, 1915) or include them only to demean both workers and their qualifications (Abbot's *Panama Canal in Picture and Prose*, 1914). Neither Pepperman nor Abbot appeared interested in much other than the United States' involvement in the canal venture and the benefits of such involvement. To this end, both drew from sources sanctioned by the Isthmian Canal Commission. For example, the title page of Abbot's book declared that it is "a complete story of Panamá, as well as the history, purpose and promise of its world-famous canal—the most gigantic engineering undertaking since the dawn of time" (p. i). This page also informs readers that the book was "approved by leading officials connected with the great enterprise" (p. i).

Abbot (1914) and Pepperman's (1915) books, as well as those by LaFeber (1989), Major (1993), and McCullough (1977), usefully explored U.S. perspectives on Panamá's independence, the construction of the canal, the canal's place in U.S. foreign policy, and the United States' status as a world power. Yet because of their orientation, not to mention the sources they used to write their narratives, their work cannot illuminate Caribbean workers' role in canal history nor the impact of this migration on Colón Men and the Caribbean region.

Three factors significantly determined how Caribbean workers registered in mainstream perspectives on the canal. First, such laborers were attractive because of their proximity to the isthmus; second, they presented a sizable population, virtually guaranteeing a constant labor supply. Third, emigration from the Caribbean was propelled by regional underemployment. Oppositional historical and geographical studies of Caribbean migration also identify economic and social reasons for Panamá migration. Senior (1978), Richardson (1985), Newton (1984), and Lewis (1980) found that overpopulation on some islands, in addition to under- and unemployment stemming from a declining Caribbean sugar industry, "pushed" many emigrants into seeking work on the isthmus.

Offering another oppositional view, Grosfoguel (1997) interpreted Caribbean migration from a historical structuralist perspective, attributing migration from peripheral Caribbean societies to "imbalances ... created by U.S. foreign capital penetration" (p. 598) and claimed that migration "occurs within a single overarching capitalist world economy wherein world systemic processes beyond the actor's control condition the migration process" (pp. 598–599). However, Thomas-Hope (1978) offered an interpretation that allows for more agency on the part of individual migrants. She claimed that migration overseas began spontaneously and at times followed patterns inconsistent with a simple explanation based on differentials of work and wages. ... Until the mid-nineteenth century, upper class experience in the Caribbean had principally been with the accumulation of wealth through plantation agriculture and trade, while the association for the mass of the population had been with slavery. The preoccupation of the post-emancipation upper class with maintaining its wealth was matched by lower class dedication to consolidating its freedom. It should not be surprising, therefore, that when their economic base was threatened by economic depression, upper class families left the islands, taking their money with them, while large scale and continuous emigration from the lower classes bore no consistent relationship either to internal or external economic trends. (p. 66)

There are differences between 19th- and 20th-century migrations to be sure; however, read in conjunction with the fictionalized Panamá migrants, it appears that West Indians migrated for labor/capitalist reasons as well as less easily quantifiable ones.

Notwithstanding the strength of the above "push factors," Newton extended Thomas-Hopes's position in claiming that West Indian Panamá migrants considered themselves masters of their fates. She said that "an important characteristic of the migrant ideology... Is that success overseas depends as much on one's luck and approach to life, as on conditions in the new environment" (p. 172). Because Newton (1984) paired "luck" with these migrants' "approach to life," she suggested that it is something that individuals can influence, if not control. One's "bad luck" in having limited opportunities at home could be changed, bringing "good luck," through isthmian migration. Some emigrants even found Panama migration educationally profitable because of their exposure to other peoples, languages, and customs. Significantly, travel "came to be regarded as a necessity in order to 'become a man,' to know the world, and to understand life. Thus emigration became highly desirable and sought after, even for its own sake" (Newton, 1984, p. 170). Moving beyond traditional analyses, exemplifed by Newton's evaluation of isthmian migration, provides more complex insights into Colón Man's motivations.

I want to emphasize that, even when pushed into leaving home because of unsatisfactory local conditions, soon-to-be Colón Men still could exert some measure of agency. A potential migrant's dissatisfaction with unfavorable economic and/or social conditions—as well as his confidence that he could change these circumstances—weighed heavily in his decision to move. During the postemancipation period, some Jamaicans and Barbadians chose to migrate to protest poor wages (Richardson, 1992, p. 183–185; Senior, 1978, p. 65). Read in this context, one can view migration as a form of resistance, as the lyrics to the following song testify:

> We want more wages, we want it now
> And if we don't get it, we going to Panama
> Yankees say they want we down there,
> We want more wages, we want it now. (Richardson, 1992, p. 132)

Richardson (1992), writing about Bajan Colón Men, claimed that this "threat" seldom brought wage increases and workers elected to migrate to Panamá. Participation in migration-as-resistance, then, fostered a particular kind of self-assurance. Through this attitude, workers demonstrated knowledge of themselves as historical actors, despite seemingly greater forces that might deter them.

Panamá Money was also a contributing factor in migrants' decisions to move. One cannot overestimate how the promise of money and material goods contributed to these workers' sense of self, one previously defined by slavery. Money earned on and remittances sent from the isthmus sometimes allowed a level of independence from plantation owners who previously had a major claim on the lives and livelihood of formerly enslaved Caribbean people. In offering the following verse, Senior (1978) revealed the extent to which Colón Men and their families felt exploited by—and liberated from—former plantation owners. These lyrics also intimate how valuable, in a nonmonetary sense, Panamá money could be:

> Mass Charley say wan' kiss Matty
> Kiss him with a willing mind
> Me ra-ra boom oh
> Colon money done (p. 89)

Continuing in this vein, McCullough (1977) claimed that the lure of Panamá money far outweighed stories about dangerous illnesses and possible death on the isthmus. Finally, money could also translate into social mobility for Colón Men from the lower classes, permitting them to purchase land and all manner of consumer goods.

Although not as measurable as cash, Panamá workers returned with skills learned through railroad and canal work—skills they would not have otherwise acquired. Senior (1978) noted that such skills translated into improved farming and building techniques in Jamaica, and Richardson (1985) stated that

> [Colón Men] made subtle but important contributions around their houses and tenantry yards, such as improving drainage in the house plots or screening windows. ... Their presence, moreover, added to the local reservoir of wisdom and knowledge about the world outside, and ... they became village elders. (p. 153)

These attitudes, possibly more than the migratory act itself, are fictionalized in Caribbean literature. In capturing them in the character of the Colón Man, creative writers confirm the value of oppositional canal histories and stories. Creative negotiations between official and alternative histories of Panamá migrants reclaim this migration experience for Colón Men as well as for the people of the region.

OPPOSITIONAL PANAMÁ NARRATIVES AS INTERPRETIVE FRAMES

Official Pana Canal histories depict Caribbean workers as an available but inefficient population. Therefore, the differences between historical and imagined/imaginary narratives raise an important question: what could transform the Panamá Canal project, unexceptional in its exploitation of Black workers, into something more complicated for Colón Men and for writers to portray them? In terms of the African American migration narrative, Griffin (1995) offered an interpretation that is useful here. With regard to Bessie Smith's blues, Griffin argued:

> Smith [uses] familiar images and rearticulates them into new forms of black cultural resistance. The images of the eagle and the Mississippi River have one meaning for the dominant, oppressor society and an altogether different meaning for the oppressed, whom [Smith] represents. (p. 21)

Consequently, the subject position of the storyteller, and the perspective from which she or he interprets "familiar images," appear to influence the substance of these images significantly. In lyrical and literary narratives about Colón Men, discussions of exploitation and denigration are replaced by more relevant descriptions. Such narratives describe Panamá Money and what it could buy, as well as Colón Men's self-assurance (often stemming from laborers' successful negotiation of myriad dangers on the isthmus). Although they might have been cheap and plentiful workers, Caribbean laborers in Panamá, as Conniff (1985) stated, routinely "considered the construction years on the canal as the heroic era, one of vast accomplishments, sacrifices, great men, camaraderie, and history-in-the-making" (p. 24).

Within a Caribbean imaginary, the figure of the Colón Man performs as one who challenges the oppressive tactics of authorities—whether they be members of the Caribbean's planter class, or canal company officials. He is successful in this role, in part, because writers who use the figure are not wedded to the "documentable" facts of his experiences. Additionally, the Colón Man appears in Caribbean literature as an enabling figure, one whose experiences and money give him knowledge that he shares with other characters. Literally speaking, such migrants are remembered fondly by friends and family (Richardson, 1985, pp. 153–154); lyrically speaking, they are sometimes satirically recalled in song (see "Panamá Man" in *Folk Songs of Barbados* by Marshall, McGeary, & Thompson, 1981). Such migrants are known throughout the region, yet by including this figure, writers are invested in more than examples of "local color." If recognized as part of each Caribbean author's writerly project, the Colón Man signifies an oppositional Caribbean identity. To put it another way, literary Colón Men can act as "signs" in much the same way "lynching" is a sign in African American migration narratives. Griffin (1995) argued that if we consider "the lynching" a sign at work in [African American] culture, then [it can be argued that] this sign is manipulated for different purposes. Initially, the sign of lynching was used by the dominant white culture of the South to evoke fear in the hearts of African-Americans and, in so doing, ... maintain the social order. ... By claiming [lynching] as part of their historical legacy, African-American artists were able to [use] the image in a variety of ways. When the image of lynching appears in the texts of African-American artists, it is not used to inflict a sense of inactivity, but instead to provoke activity: either it is a catalyst to northern migration or it provides the foundation for staking a racial claim on the South. (p. 47)

Griffin (1995) argued that the lynching-as-sign is not merely intended to project white supremacy and black victimization into African American creative texts. Rather, the sign remembers a complex claim on the Southern landscape and foregrounds a decisive moment of black agency. Notably, this agency can take the form of migration—a physical movement evocative of a shift in consciousness from black victim to black agent. Caribbean writers similarly deploy images of the Panamá Canal worker. By examining the literary migrant's complex nature, one can uncover such writers' representational ambitions.

Land, money, Pan-Africanism, and cosmopolitanism define Thelwell's Colón Man, Maas' Nattie; read in relation to the protagonist, this figure also enacts a sociopolitical reorientation. The relationship between Maas' Nattie and Ivan enables the latter's formation of an activist identity. Nattie imparts to Ivan/Rhygin the value of a Pan-Africanist worldview, of Jamaican peasant culture, and of tradition. The boy draws on this relationship and the identity it calls for to respond to circumstances that he finds oppressive: urban poverty, exploitation by upper-class Jamaicans and Jamaican government officials, and the overwhelming influence of U.S. culture. Because of who Nattie is and what he represents in the novel, he supports Ivan/Rhygin in his active and violent response to exploitation. In Rhygin, Thelwell thus promotes an activist subjectivity derived from rural and working-class urban experiences.

MAKING RHYGIN, MAKING A RADICAL JAMAICAN IDENTITY

The Harder They Come documents Ivan's rich culture and the centrality of a history that privileges the land, family, community, and a strong sense of self. Maas' Nattie provides a necessary link in this chain and exerts a particular influence on the boy. He gives Ivan a larger context into which his personal experiences—pre- and post-Kingston—can be placed. The strongly held and practiced folk traditions that Thelwell documents in Ivan's pre-Kingston world explicitly connect to Rhygin's life in the city. This supports my interpretation not only of Thelwell's inclusion of Ivan's past, but also of the continuing influence Nattie has on the boy, even after he leaves his village. Kingston adds to Ivan's experiences by exposing him to a culture largely defined by U.S. films and tourist dollars. Ivan ends up a member of Kingston's "rude bwai" community, one that patterns itself after U.S. Western movies and Jamaican "roots" music. Through a series of confrontations with "progress," Ivan becomes Rhygin: infamous for killing four police officers and, with the help of Kingston's "suffrahs," existing outside of an oppressive authority longer than believed possible.[2] Although the police eventually kill Rhygin, the identity he espouses and the popular movement he initiates does not die.

The character of Nattie, in and of itself, does not transform the exploitative systems he encounters; he thrives, but offers no overt resistance to them. Yet it is through his influence that the protagonist's revolution becomes possible. In offering this reading, I foreground the importance of a Jamaican reality that is shaped by contrasts and the identity that results from such contrasts. Examinations of slavery and colonialism, and creative disruptions of their legacies, frequently appear in Caribbean literature. In *Abeng*, for example, Cliff (1984) wrote of the Jamaican town of Runaway Bay where, months before the official end to slavery, a slave owner sets fire to 100 enslaved people. Yet Cliff's narrator remembers this brutality differently:

> The bones of dead slaves made the land at Runaway Bay rich and green. Tall royal palms lined the avenue leading to the houses of the development. Breadfruit trees, branches fat with their deep green lobed leaves, created shade around the stucco bungalows. The breeze from the sea came through the windows of the houses and made the walls taste of salt. (p. 40)

Images of white masters and black slaves, relationships between violence and oppression, and African Jamaicans' resultant claim to the land, merge to form the basis of a contemporary Jamaican reality. Cliff (1984) attributed the landscape's fertility to the bodies—and labor—of enslaved people and brings the simultaneity of the past (Jamaica's history of slavery and brutality) and the present (the current reality of the landscape and African Jamaicans' continuing stake in it) to the fore. She fictionally reintroduced links between African Jamaicans, slavery, and the land, remembering their heritage of enslavement, a history effaced by a colonial educational system and forgotten by those convinced of their own "otherness." Much as Griffin (1995) argued for the re-visionary value of the sign of lynching in African American migration narratives, Cliff assessed the value of an alternative vision of Jamaican history. Though victimized by slavery, Cliff does not represent *Abeng's* Jamaicans.

---

[2] Significant to the novel but outside the scope of this essay is Thelwell's critique of "progress" in Jamaica. Ivan, some years after he leaves the country, returns to find everything changed. His ancestral home has returned to bush, taking his family's burial ground with it. Maas' Nattie's farm has been claimed by White American "Ras Tafarian warriors." Village land is being mined for bauxite, and the mining process covers the once lush landscape with rust-colored slime. The people of his youth have moved on or died, or are co-opted by U.S. tourist money.

Thelwell similarly recuperates Jamaica's rural and working-class urban populations, for he sees in them not only the strength to withstand victimization but also the capacity to "re-vision" the urban landscape. By documenting Ivan's life prior to his arrival in Kingston, the author makes clear his interest in the revolutionary possibilities of Jamaican country people and, specifically, this group's ability to confront an urban culture overly focused on the Unites States. With this in mind, Rhygin—although a murderer—is not merely a criminal; his existence outside the law can be read as a rejection of debilitating Western and upper-class influences.[3] Because the author draws a strong correlation between Ivan's upbringing and Rhygin's behavior, one must recognize the former as enabling—or at least supporting—the latter. Therefore, *The Harder They Come* champions the revolutionary features of Jamaican folk and working-class cultures. Interestingly, Nattie serves as a vehicle through which the author effectively represents these ideas.

The Colón Man shares his blended historical and creative personas with Ivan. The author intends his novel to disrupt the tourist's vision of Jamaica and, at the same time, to propagate its revolutionary message for a Jamaican audience. To these ends, he imbues the film's Ivan, already existing as a Creole, with mythic, popular, and historic truths. Thelwell (1991) noted that "[Jamaican] history [is] riddled with, depending on your point of view, either rebel heroes or ungrateful, blood-thirsty savages. A contemporary incarnation of that figure, one Ivanhoe "Rhygin" Martin, captured Henzell's cinematic imagination" (p. 140). Henzell's protagonist, Ivan Martin, blends singer Jimmy Cliff's personal history (Cliff left rural Jamaica to become a singer and was exploited by a record company executive) and that of 1940s Jamaican outlaw Ivanhoe "Rhygin" Martin; "thus the central figure of the film conflated, in effect, two ghetto-culture heroes: the outlaw badman and the reggae musician" (p. 144). The process through which the novel's protagonist comes to exist as representative of a particular Caribbean subjectivity mimics the historical reality of the region.

The novel's protagonist is composed of various aspects of the real and the fictional; Thelwell continues Ivan's creolization by linking him to Jamaica's Maroons as well as to African and Pan-African warriors. Ivan, as a member of Jamaica's rude bwai community, also represents an urban, roots culture that is influenced by U.S. films, reggae music, and the Rastafarian religion. Thelwell thus weaves historical truths, popular and cultural realities, and political commentary into his novelistic vision of a Jamaican peasantry.

---

[3] Thelwell (1991) noted that

> not only was [the film *The Harder They Come*] Jamaican in story, theme, social issues, and music ... it was *working-class* Jamaican in language and point of view—so much so, in fact, that it is deeply resented to this day by the more backward and shallow elements of the middle classes there, in whose view it projects the wrong image of the country. (p. 136)

Ivan identifies Maas' Nattie as a Colón Man in terms that speak of the latter's physical superiority, intelligence, and position within their community. The novel quickly establishes the older man as self-sufficient and as a strong influence on Ivan. Nattie migrates to earn money and status, two of the most typical reasons given by Caribbean migrants to Panamá. Maas' Nattie first travels to Cuba and performs agricultural work; he moves on to Panamá because he hears that he can earn more money. Returning to Jamaica, the Colón Man invests his earning in a farm, then continues his migrations for another 25 years.

Because of his travels, Nattie has no family; Ivan, therefore, is his "son." Thinking about the older man, Ivan reflects that "he liked Maas' Nattie, who was the richest black man in the district" (p. 38). Here, the boy respectfully recalls Nattie's achievements on the Panamanian isthmus even though, evidenced in the opening epigraph, he does not know what a canal is. Nattie's migrations, the money he made, and his experiences could easily have separated him from his community, but the opposite occurs. He becomes part of the village as an elder, adviser, and contributor to its lore. However, the esteem in which the villagers hold him is not uncomplicated. The novel reveals this during a communal corn harvest held at Nattie's house:

> Maas' Nattie's mind would wander [after a few drinks] and he would utter phrases in different languages picked up in the travels of his youth. A couple of Spanish sentences might conclude with Marcus Garvey's "Rise up ye mighty race and accomplish what ye will." Each interjection was met with admiring murmurs since talking in tongues was much respected as a sign of wisdom. (p. 59)

The specifics of Nattie's wisdom do not appear to be important to the villagers. They respect that Nattie has knowledge, but only as far as it fits into their already established ways of knowing. To put it another way, they understand and appreciate the phenomenon of speaking in tongues; the villagers do not, however, examine the import and meaning of Nattie's specific knowledge of Marcus Garvey in the context of their present circumstances.

However, the novel demonstrates that Nattie's influence on Ivan empowers the boy, encouraging him to know himself as part of a history of revolutionary struggle. Nattie tells Ivan stories:

> About Cudjo the maroon warrior and Ma Nannie his sister who was a witch and a warrior too, and about the great Marcus Garvey who was 'the black man savior.' ... Maas' Nattie never told Anancy stories or talked about duppi and evil spirits, but spoke of real black men like King Prempeh and King Chaka, and Ras Menelik whose black armies defeated the Italians and took back his country which was in Africa. (pp. 38–39)

The import of the Colón Man's stories is very specific. His tales are about African and Jamaican people in active confrontation with foreign enemies. Nattie's black people are not passive victims of history, nor are they defeated by an inability to act in their own behalf. The thrust of his stories is also Pan-Africanist as he positions Nannie and Cudjo in a tradition of revolutionaries. Cudjo, Ma Nannie, Garvey, Prempeh, Chaka, and Menelik were individuals fighting with and for their communities. That Nattie, perceived of as wise because of his travels, tells these tales, adds weight to their meanings. Ivan learns to appreciate individuals-in-communities as agents in historical struggles against foreign domination. Finally, although he comments that Nattie tells tales about "real men" rather than about ghosts and evil spirits, suggesting that he finds "duppi" stories unbelievable, he receives Ma Nannie's witchcraft without comment. Ivan's exposure to the spiritual traditions of Jamaican people generally, and specifically to those of his village, coexists with his historical education; I believe this interrelationship enables Ivan to value each form of knowledge. Thus Nattie's stories offer the protagonist a template for an activist Jamaican identity.

The Colón Man grooms Ivan in the traditions of his ancestors and in a particular relationship to land and history; the boy, however, translates these lessons through his own vision. It is this view, what Nattie calls the Maroon spirit of the boy's grandfather, that makes Ivan more than a cipher. Others join Nattie in remarking on Ivan's specialness, saying "there was something about Ivan that fit the name Rhygin. He was so full of life and energy, so full of questions. There was nothing that didn't interest him, and nothing that he didn't think he could master" (p. 17).[4] Although the Colón Man espouses his own activist politics, *The Harder They Come* suggests that his ways are his—specific to his experiences. Ivan, encountering different "enemies," succeeds in facing them because he has the benefit of Maas' Nattie's vision. The protagonist creolizes Nattie's lessons by accommodating them to his current reality; to put it another way, the boy does not uncritically absorb the older man's experiences. In accordance with the Maroon spirit of his grandfather and his life in Kingston, Rhygin's "self" is cosmopolitan and embraces Pan-Africanism and Jamaica's cultural influences.

Although Ivan reads Nattie's lessons through his own sense of the world, he continues to hold the older man in high regard. The boy develops a taste for Kingston after hearing some "town" music at a local café; he is then determined to go to town and become a singer. On the eve of Ivan's journey, Nattie reinforces Ivan's relationships to family and land. Nattie moves through Ivan's homestead, pointing out the gravesites of the latter's grandparents and uncles. The Colón Man tells the boy, "you come from somewhe', from decent people dem, people whe' nevah ha' no heap a money—but dem nevah poor neider. And you raise up decent, to know what right an' to have manners. Bwai, don't grow 'way from you raisin,' eh?" (p. 110). The old man seeks to ground Ivan and help him navigate his present

---

[4] Thelwell used the definition of *rhygin* from Cassidy and LePage's 1967 *Dictionary of Jamaican English*. It defines *rhygin* as an adjective meaning "spirited, vigorous, lively, passionate with great vitality and force; aggressive. Probably a form of [the] English 'raging.'"

and future. With this, Nattie heads off. Although he never "physically" appears in the novel again, his influence continues to be apparent.

Thelwell laces references to Nattie throughout the remainder of the novel, reinforcing the character's influence. For example, Ivan reads his first experience outside of the village through one of Nattie's stories. While on the Kingston-bound bus, Ivan passes a cane field in flames. The only context he has for interpreting this scene is "Maas' Nattie's stories of slaves in revolt burning down the plantations" (p. 112). Ivan knows there are "no more slaves" and continues to wonder about the fire until another passenger enlightens him:

> Is just burn dem a burn off de leaf dem. Mek it easier fe cut de cane.
> Den, it no burn up de cane too?
> Dem say it no harm it. But sometime when de workers dem strike, or if dem have some dispute dem will burn up de cane still. (p. 113)

Ivan thinks Nattie will be pleased to know that, in response to "some dispute," the "black man was still a burn down the canefields" (p. 113). This quote demonstrates that the boy does not leave his country-based knowledge behind. His history lives with him; more importantly, it also shapes the ways he sees the present. The newness of his experiences excites him, but does not replace or topple the coherence of his rural life. Again, this passage establishes Nattie's association with an activist tradition, one in which black people—enslaved and free—fight against oppression and exploitation. Ivan has learned the Colón Man's lessons about the strength of community and personal activism.

Excitement colors Ivan's trip to Kingston. On arrival, however, he quickly confronts much of what Nattie warned him against. Ivan falls victim to the city: he is robbed, jobless, and homeless for his first few months in Kingston.[5] At his lowest point, Ivan defines himself solely in terms of his current poverty and the self-image he absorbs from Kingston's middle and upper class blacks. This is a point where Nattie's stories fail Ivan; in the old man's tales, blacks confronted "foreign," easily identifiable enemies. Ivan cannot see blacks from the middle class as enemies and thus cannot filter their view of him. Instead, he "could feel a shrinking, a constriction, a closing up and sealing off of something that had always been part of him" (p. 170).

Ultimately, a familiar "something" rescues Ivan from his poverty and alienation from self. Hungry, Ivan tries to steal fruit from a market woman. She catches him but sees in him something more than thief. Even in his degraded state, the woman recognizes him as a kindred spirit, one born of a familiar relationship to

---

[5] In many ways, Thelwell used Kingston as a metaphor for colonialism, neocolonialism, and classism. The author, although cognizant of what motivates rural-to-urban migration, exhibits a preference for Jamaica's rural communities. Traditions of this population, according to Thelwell, foster a self-reliance and reliance on community that sustains Ivan when he is faced with the debilitating effects of urban life.

"country." She says she can see that "is not here [Ivan] belong" (p. 176). The market woman gives him food and tells him that "because a man sleep ina fowl-nest, it doan mean say fowl-nest is 'im bed" (p. 176). These words give Ivan the strength he needs. He recalls his old self, but his experience of Kingston forces him to move beyond his history as well as Nattie's experiences. It is not insignificant that immediately after his interaction with the market woman Ivan remembers a job opportunity. Their encounter propels the protagonist closer to becoming "rhygin/Rhygin": working as a handyman for Preacher, Ivan earns money, falls in love with Elsa, and records his song "The Harder They Come."

Working for Preacher gives Ivan money to frequent the cinema. At his first show, he finds "young, black, poor, 'suffrahs' and the children of 'suffrahs,' they constituted an audience so rapt and attentive, so impressionable and apparently uncritical that their identification [with film characters] was almost total" (p. 147). Ivan learns something else:

> The world of the movie was harsh and brutal, yes. But it was also one where justice, once aroused, was more elemental and deadly than all the hordes of evil. He thought Maas' Nattie would approve of such a world. (p. 149)

Considering Ivan's sense of justice, his attraction to the movies (particularly Westerns) is clear. Ivan soon comes to be known as Rhygin among the cinema's rude bwais, many of whom take the names of their favorite film characters: Bogart, George Raft, Hitler (p. 195). Note, however, that Ivan's nickname is uniquely Jamaican, while his peers take the names of U.S. actors. Although Ivan is as drawn to these American films as the other suffrahs, Thelwell makes Ivan's attraction clear: The young man believes in a justice that is stronger than evil. He is not merely taken in by the glamor of U.S. culture.

After Ivan enters into Kingston's rude bwai community, he invokes Nattie two more times. In both cases, the relationship to Nattie leaves Ivan dissatisfied. The first occurs when a group of Rastafarians attempts to "take" Kingston and purge it of its spirit of colonialism; city police quickly disperse the demonstration (p. 209). Ivan also "sees" Nattie in the spiritual convictions of a Rastafarian named Peter. Each reference suggests aspects of Nattie's stories and personality, but what Ivan finds lacking is the Colón Man's revolutionary directive, the component of his tales and his personal migration experiences that encourage people to act in accordance with their own best interests. Ivan—shaped by Nattie, the Maroon spirit of his grandfather, and his stay in Kingston—wants more than the symbolism the Rastafarians offer and more than Ras Peter's passive spirituality. The current climate in Kingston seems to demand more.

Ivan and a friend comment on that climate and conclude that the people are more bitter than before. They attribute this bitterness to the negative effects of tourism, an abusive police force, and crippling poverty. Rastafarianism and reggae/roots music relieve the pressure of some of these stressors; still, Ivan's background gives him access to stories that offer more than alleviation. His violent and justified response to an attempted assassination by police demonstrates his more than symbolic, active response against injustice.

Ivan is marked for death because he refuses to pay Jose, a police informant charged with controlling Kingston's ganja traders, for "protection." In retaliation, Jose enlists the police to execute Ivan. Ivan escapes, however, and kills several police officers in the process. "Ivan" no longer exists after he kills these policemen; he is now Rhygin:

> The feeling of power and invincibility flooded him again. Star-bwai can' dead! Star-bwai can' dead! [Peter], Maas' Nattie unu no see! Ras Suffrah look! Babylon get a blow! (p. 349)

The *star-bwai,* previously defined as a film's male lead, is a term that alludes to Rhygin's identification with U.S. films. At his first town movie, Ivan learns that the lead cannot die. However, where these imported films feature white men from the United States, Rhygin's drama features a Jamaican. Such films influence him, but Ivan can nonetheless insert himself in the role of lead. As the police pressure marijuana traders to turn Rhygin in, we see that this "outlaw" vindicates this community, one oppressed by poverty and lack of opportunity, and manipulated for the benefit of the upper classes. They, consequently, protect Rhygin, for he strikes a blow and speaks for each of them. Where the rude bwais used to mimic heroes from U.S. western and gangster movies, they now have Rhygin. For them, he functions as the heroes from Nattie's stories do for Ivan: Rhygin struggles against, and bests, Babylon. Rhygin's place in Kingston urban community marks the evolution of Nattie's influence; rather than an individual as an agent within a system of power, Rhygin addresses the system itself. Through actions enabled by an activist identity, he finds the justice he has long been seeking.

"The Harder They Come," the song Ivan records for the corrupt record producer, Mr. Hilton, represents Ivan's creolized persona:

> The ... song had an assertive and rebellious spirit heightened by the up-beat semireggae rhythm Hilton put around it. The words were only one element—the voice was good, rich toned and flexible, easy with the music—but the total effect was a combination, a fusion of words, melody, and rhythm into a passionate affirmation of a vision as hard, resistant, stubbornly desperate and macho as shantytown itself.

> Ah say
> De harder dey come
> Is de harder dey fall
> One and aall
> But I'd raddah be a free man in mah grave
> Dan living as a puppet or a slave
> So, as sure as the sun will shine
> I'm gonna get mine. (p. 281)

In becoming rhygin/Rhygin, Ivan dramatizes the identity that his nickname suggests. Nattie's teachings and Ivan's Maroon spirit, combined with the communities of which he becomes part in Kingston, authorize Rhygin's rebellion. All of Kingston's dwellers can claim Rhygin and celebrate his exploits. Sightings of him and tales about his feats proliferate and are documented by graffiti that appears all over the city: "Rhygin was here/But 'im jus' disappear!" (p. 356). He is a local figure who challenges prescribed roles for poor and working-class Jamaicans. Rhygin asserts his selfhood and dignity and, simultaneously, undermines the authority of those in power. Ivan, once inconsequential in the purview of the powerful, makes himself consequential—and thus removes himself from their habitual way of seeing and legislating him.

Elsa eventually turns Rhygin in, and the police kill him as he attempts to board a ship to Cuba (p. 390). Although Rhygin is physically absent from the remainder of the novel—like Nattie—the author makes it clear that Rhygin has become an integral part of the consciousness of the people of Kingston. Hearing the end of Rhygin's song on the radio, a boy muses:

> "Wait," the boy said. "Ah t'ink dem ban dah song de?" But he had little time to wonder. He had to deal with more urgent matters, the approach of the posse.
>
> "Bram, Bram, Bram!" He leapt from cover, guns blazing.
>
> The posse returned fire. "You dead!" the sheriff shouted. "Cho man, you dead!"
>
> "Me Ah Rhygin!" the boy shouted back. "Me can' dead!" (pp. 391–392)

The Harder They Come ends with these boys playing "Rhygin." Where the rude bwais previously reenacted U.S. cowboy movies, these young boys now perform Rhygin's life. U.S. culture shapes the experiences of the former group; the latter, however, looks to a Jamaican hero. Ivan/Rhygin is an outlaw-hero-revolutionary who replaces the heroes of U.S. films; he reorients the identity of Kingston's suffrahs toward home.

CONCLUSIONS

I do not believe that Thelwell is fully conscious of his Colón Man; in other words, I believe that the figure's contribution to *The Harder They Come* becomes evident through interpretation. My examination of historical versions of the figure, compared to its creative representations, demonstrates that literary Colón Men often echo an author's goal for his work. Thelwell is a writer who is particularly useful in this context, for he has defined a "West Indian writer," and outlined such a writer's role in revisioning Caribbean identity and history. *The Harder They Come*, read through Maas' Nattie's influence, reflects its author's revolutionary vision for Caribbean subjectivity.

Despite adverse conditions faced by West Indian workers in Panamá, in the Caribbean imaginary these workers are financial successes as well as social and political activists. Literary Colón Men magnify these workers' often silent voices, ones that articulate the ways they responded to exploitation, as well as how they achieved their goals, and earned and used their Panamá money. Caribbean writers tap into imagined representations of Colón Man to reinvent the figure's experiences, to tell other histories and stories, and to foreground the influential role of culture in Caribbean peoples' sense of self and responses to oppression.

It is important to note that fictional Panamá migrants do not merely celebrate oppositional Caribbean histories and identities, nor do they solely inspire positive action. These literary figures are as complicated as the circumstances from which they evolved. Official histories of the canal document French and U.S. goals and achievements, but historians of the Caribbean insert Colón Men's alternative histories and stories into these official versions. Though they feature descriptions of accidental death, disease, and racism, they also offer examples of self-transformation, survival, and success. Creative narratives feature Panamá migrants who are elders, lovers, cosmopolitan and politically astute. I see the relation between these versions of the migrant's reality as a complex negotiation that reveals much about the lived experience of Caribbean people, a reality that binds together cultural, historical, and social truths with the realities of colonialism/imperialism, economics, geography, and migration. Literary renditions of the figure's reality, therefore, are not merely derived from the figure's "actual" experiences; rather, literary Colón Men are derived from truths other than those determined by official and unofficial histories, exploitations, and oppressions.

REFERENCES

Abbot, W. J. (1914). *Panama and the canal in picture and prose*. London: Syndicate.
Bryce-Laporte, R. (1982). Preface. In W. F. Stinner, K. de Albuquerque, & R. Bryce-Laporte (Eds.), *Return migration and remittances: Developing a Caribbean perspective* (RIIES Occasional Papers No. 3). Washington, DC: Smithsonian Institution.
Cassidy, F. G., & LePage, R. B. (1967). *Dictionary of Jamaican English*. New York: Cambridge University Press.
Christian, B. (1987, Spring). The race for theory. *Culture Critique, 6*, 53.
Cliff, M. (1984). *Abeng*. New York: Penguin.
Conniff, M. L. (1985). *Black labor on a White canal: Panama, 1904–1981*. Pittsburgh, PA: University of Pittsburgh Press.
Dance, D. C. (1984/1992). *New World Adams: Conversations with contemporary West Indian writers*. London: Peepal.
Glissant, E. (1989). *Caribbean discourse: Selected essays* (J. M. Dash, Trans.). Charlottesville: University of Virginia Press.
Griffin, F. J. (1995). *"Who set you flowin?": The African American migration narrative*. New York: Oxford University Press.

Grosfoguel, R. (1997). Colonial Caribbean migrations to France, the Netherlands, Great Britain and the United States. *Ethnic and Racial Studies, 20,* 594–612.
Henzell, P. (1973) *The harder they come* [Film]. International Films.
LaFeber, W. (1989). *The Panama Canal: The crisis in historical perspective.* New York: Oxford University Press.
Lamming, G. (1983). *In the castle of my skin.* New York: Schocken.
Lewis, L. (1980). *The West Indian in Panama: Black labor in Panama, 1850–1914.* Washington, DC: University Press of America.
Major, J. (1993). *Prize possession: The United States and the Panama Canal, 1903–1979.* New York: Cambridge University Press.
Marshall, T., McGeary, P., & Thompson, G. (Eds.). (1981). *Folk songs of Barbados.* Bridgetown, Barbados: MacMarson.
McCullough, D. (1977). *The path between the seas: The creation of the Panama Canal, 1870–1914.* New York: Simon & Schuster.
Newton, V. (1984). *The silver men: West Indian labour migration to Panama, 1850–1914.* Mona, Jamaica: University of the West Indies, Institute of Social and Economic Research.
Pepperman, W. L. (1915). *Who built the Panama Canal?* London: Dent.
Richardson, B. (1985). *Panama money in Barbados, 1900–1920.* Knoxville: University of Tennessee Press.
Richardson, B. (1992). *The Caribbean in the wider world, 1492–1992: A regional geography.* Cambridge, England: Cambridge University Press.
Senior, O. (1978). "The Colon people." *Jamaica Journal, 12,* 87–103.
Thelwell, M. (1980/1988). *The harder they come.* New York: Grove.
Thelwell, M. (1991). The harder they come: From film to novel. *Grand Street, 10,* 135–165.
Thomas-Hope, E. (1978). The establishment of a migration tradition: British West Indian movements to the Hispanic Caribbean in the century after emancipation. In C. G. Clarke (Ed.), *Caribbean social relations* (pp. 66–81). London: University of Liverpool, Centre for Latin American Studies.

The Geopolitics of Identity: Popular Literature, Censorship, and the Spanish Media

Mireya Folch-Serra
Department of Geography
University of Western Ontario

National identity and manufactured unity have paved the way to the modern phenomenon of the nation–state, which emerged around the French Revolution in the late 18th century. The nation–state sought to unite the people by means of homogenization, creating a "common culture, symbols, values, reviving traditions and myths of origin, and sometimes inventing them" (Guibernau, 2000, p. 989). Ethnic division had no place or explanation in this product of the Enlightenment. Yet, despite the high minded aim of nation builders, ethnic and cultural differences did not disappear overnight. Indeed, they have been noted and written about by reporters and political observers alike. Their vision of these differences challenges the status quo in many ways, and most likely has altered the manner in which national unity is perceived inside and outside national borders.

The powerful myth of national unity is one of those constructions that has been defended with extreme vigor by its custodians in many parts of the world. Mythic thought operates in a unique way. Whenever the mind asks itself what signification is, as in the meaning of *national identity,* for example, a "true" signification must always be found. To sustain this belief, polemical elements, such as ethnic divisions or cultural differences, tend not to be sanctioned by the social imagination, nor recognized as components of the body politic, lest they deflate the wholesomeness of the manufactured fiction of national unity.

National identity and manufactured unity have paved the way to the modern phenomenon of the nation–state, which emerged around the French Revolution in the late 18th century. The nation–state sought to unite the people by means of ho-

---

Requests for reprints should be sent to Mireya Folch-Serra, Department of Geography, University of Western Ontario, London, Ontario, Canada N6A 5C2. E-mail: folch@uwo.ca

mogenization, creating a "common culture, symbols, values, reviving traditions and myths of origin, and sometimes inventing them" (Guibernau, 2000, p. 989). Ethnic division had no place or explanation in this product of the Enlightenment. Yet, despite the high minded aim of nation builders, ethnic and cultural differences did not disappear overnight. Indeed, they have been noted and written about by reporters and political observers alike. Their vision of these differences challenges the status quo in many ways, and most likely has altered the manner in which national unity is perceived inside and outside national borders.

How do popular authors and press commentators view national minorities and ethnic conflict? To whom are the roles of winners and losers, victors and victims assigned? Do narratives influence public opinion? Can the media sway the general understanding of the geopolitics of identity?

I explore these questions through the analysis of Tom Clancy's best-seller *Op-Center: Balance of Power* (Clancy & Pieczenik, 1998), a thriller depicting a sequel of the Spanish Civil War. The novel's Spanish translation (Clancy, 1999), however, differs from the author's original. The Spanish version sought to sanitize so-called inexact geographical and historical facts, and supposedly bring the text closer to "reality." Are these alterations an isolated occurrence? Do they have antecedents? What follows is an examination of the semantics of translation, the context in which contemporary Spanish publishing takes place, and the unintended outcome of revisions.

GEOPOLITICS AND FICTION

Cold War politics are becoming almost a legendary representation of the times when certainty clearly differentiated right from wrong and allowed most people to decide where to place their allegiance. Consequently, Cold War narratives were built around well-defined scenarios and ignored altogether issues of liminality, ambiguity, and skepticism. Like those in fairy tales, heroes and villains would be created as good or evil without shades in between. However, after the 1989 Eastern revolutions and the 1990 fall of the Berlin Wall, the apparent coherence of the Cold War began to fall apart (see Dodds, 1998). The world dissolved into competing regional powers and interests, and mass media had to provide more imaginative reconceptualizations of international relations and cast off the older ways of understanding global politics (Sharp, 1998). Writers such as John le Carré and Tom Clancy embraced the new reality and began to create offbeat images of identity and geopolitical relations. In this new global context, Clancy searched into the past and found inspiration in the Spanish Civil War. His version of it, nonetheless, has little to do with the ideological struggle of 1936–1939. Instead, he summons issues more akin to current news reports such as ethnic conflict, terrorism, and corruption.

Although the media's impact on international relations has not been entirely recognized, its influence on state practice remains a strong factor. This can be detected in the construction of hegemonic cultural values that shape both the actions of politicians and the expectations of societies (Sharp, 1998). As will become evident in this article, when a work of fiction is perceived as a disturbing geopolitical agent, the custodians of cultural values take on the task of altering its content. Clancy's novel is a case in point, but it is not the only one. In Spain the practice of editing and censoring has a long authoritarian tradition.[1] The questions proposed earlier are meant to frame the backbone of my argument and help me demonstrate that after a long period of repression, some institutions of the body politic remain conditioned by habits of the past.

The protagonists of Clancy's *Balance of Power* are Spain's main ethnic groups, mostly Basques, Catalans, and Castilians, matched by American undercover agents who, in the late 1990s, struggle to prevent an ensuing episode of the Spanish Civil War. These ethnic factions, who also fight among themselves, represent a menace to the state. As a result of being divided among the groups and threatened by the Mafia, Spain is plunged into a profound crisis, which is promptly detected by U.S. military intelligence. Agents are sent to deflect the danger of civil war and to find out who the conspirators are. They detect that the Catalans want control of the state through a bellicose alliance with the Basques, who, through this political payoff, will obtain their independence. Under these conditions, the state becomes the victim while minority nationalism is portrayed as unlawful activities dominated by terrorist operations and characterized by corruption. Although Clancy's imagination provides an abundance of improbable, far-fetched situations, fact and fiction become nonetheless indistinguishable in real time and space. Terrorist attacks are actually widespread in Spain. According to the latest polls, Spaniards consider terrorism to be their biggest problem; one that has brought about a climate of fear, despondence, and civil war flashbacks.[2]

HISTORICAL MEMORY AND THE SPANISH CIVIL WAR

January 1999 marked the 60th anniversary of the end of the Spanish Civil War, an intense conflict that generated an exodus of about a half million refugees and produced countless fatalities. This war, considered the European war of the century because it exposed, for the first time, the fundamental clash between fascism and

---

[1] Another instance of idiosyncratic censorship involving George Orwell's *Homage to Catalonia* (1952) has been reported in an editorial note published in *Babelia*, the literary supplement of *El País*, 2001, March 17, page 2 (no author). I have corroborated that the book is still sold by main publishers such as Ariel, Seix Barral, and Circulo de Lectores with the same expurgated and censored translation of 1970, which was the first year in which Franco's regime allows its publication (see Orwell, G. 1985; 1970, *Homenaje a Cataluña*, Traductor Carlos Pujol. Barcelona: Editorial Seix Barral.
[2] Juliá (2001), among other commentators, feared that "shadows of the past" could unleash a new bloody conflict in contemporary Spain (*El País*, 2001, February 18, p. 27).

communism, paradoxically has had little lasting resonance for the Spanish people. In fact, the very first historical combatants against fascism were Spanish Republicans, yet little recognition was given to them in Spain and in the world at large for the duration of the Cold War. A cloak of oblivion covered the period encompassing the years of the Republic and the Civil War, prompting Hooper, correspondent in Spain for *The Guardian*, to observe in 1995 that the locals did not "forgive and forget, they just forgot" (p. 78). An attitude made easier by Franco's death in 1975 and the fact that his reign was equated with backwardness.

To make their country modern, Spaniards felt they would have to cast aside the dictator's legacy entirely (Bradley, 1999), and alongside the memories of repression, they also dismissed the democratic legacy of the Republican years. The results of this collective amnesia are well recognized by contemporary Spanish scholars. For at least 40 years, little was done in Spain to research and write about the Civil War (Juliá, 1999; Preston, 1999). The perception of the defeated Republicans as enemies, traitors, masons, atheists, anarchists, and communists continued to feed the propaganda machinery of Franco's dictatorship for a long time. Even Vilar (1986), the paramount French historian of Spanish economy and culture, did not publish his account of the war until several decades had passed, but his book did at least commemorate its 50th anniversary.[3] Ironically, this peculiar Spanish neglect of their own recent history stands in huge contrast to the enormous bibliography produced over the years by foreign scholars and journalists.[4]

It was foreigners who kept alive the theorization of memory in Spain.[5] Their research, coupled with a large taxonomy of ways of remembering, has become indispensable in writing modern history, explaining the unfolding of conflict between states, and pondering the meaning of national identity. Historical memory is not just an academic exercise; it functions to hold back the course of oblivion (see Boyarin, 1994; Connerton, 1989; Gillis, 1994; Halbwachs, 1950, 1925/1994; Hobsbawm & Ranger, 1983; Le Goff, 1988; Llobera, 1996; Nora, 1984; Todorov, 1995). Its marks on the cultural landscape, dubbed *lieux de mémoire,* keep memory alive, as in the case of concentration camps, Hiroshima, and what is left of the Berlin Wall, charged with ominous meanings. Other emblematic "sites of memory" are the typical monuments of French towns that commemorate the fallen in the two great wars and con-

---

[3] It is a striking fact that the socialist government of Felipe González refused to acknowledge the defense of democracy by the defeated government of the Republic in the 50th anniversary of the Civil War. More recently, the "Partido Popular" (the party in power) also refused to condemn the crimes committed by the dictatorship, an issue copiously commented by the Spanish Press (see for example Eduardo Haro Tecglen's Visto/Oido: No condenar, *El País,* 2001, May 24, p. 53.
[4] Even a *London Times* correspondent expressed that for Spaniards to learn what happened to them 60 years ago, they have to read the accounts of the British (Juliá, 1999, p. 48).
[5] Some classical works, such as Orwell's (1952), Plenn's (1946), Thomas's (1986), Pike Wingeate's (1993), and Preston's (1993, 1995, 1999), stand out in the huge body of literature devoted to the Civil War.

vey feelings of patriotic pride. In Spain, all memories of the democratic period between 1931 and 1939 (the years of the Second Republic) were obliterated, and no sites of commemoration were left standing anywhere. On the other side, the monuments erected by Franco's regime to celebrate his Catholic crusade became ubiquitous in plazas and streets that also had a name change (Madalena, 1996).[6]

There is an abundance of compiled sites and narratives whose examination illustrates the intricacies of historical and collective memory (Alted, 1996; Candau, 1998). I do believe, however, that the indispensable antithesis of memory is less considered. Although collective and historical memory have been employed generation after generation to build consensus about the past, there are other instances where events are silenced, distorted, and relegated to oblivion. As a concept, *oblivion* should be detailed just as much as memory, because there are also different ways and kinds of forgetting—from the simple voluntary individual decision to forget, to those ways imposed deliberately and systematically by political design on a collective. Oblivion can be established by edict (Veyne, 1978). It is not an unusual occurrence; it happened in ancient times when the defunct emperor's name was erased from archival documents and from monuments' inscriptions. This was the practice of *damnatio memoriae,* which in the recent past has been applied to a variety of cases (see Loraux, 1997). For example, the 1915 Armenian genocide now rescued from oblivion after 85 years, by France's official recognition. Or the case of Chile, where about 25 years have been required to dig out, literally and metaphorically, the *desaparecidos* remains to recuperate General Pinochet's intentionally hidden past. In Spain, it has taken 60 years after the end of the Civil War in 1939 for Spanish authorities to begin to recognize, and Spanish scholars to fully investigate, Republican times and the circumstances of the Civil War.

The government of the Second Spanish Republic, elected on April 14, 1931, was never defeated in the urns. It was challenged by a coup d'état and a declaration of war broadcast by the factious band on July 18, 1936 (Abellán, 1983; García Jiménez, 1980). The war produced a set of different discourses manifested in propaganda posters, editorial pages of newspapers, and religious pastorals. On the side of the rebels, the symbol was a religious crusade; for the Republicans, it was social justice. Both sides fought to the death defending their principles, and the struggle initiated a geopolitical strategy from the outset of the war.

---

[6]To date, the symbols of Franco's dictatorship continue to pervade the Spanish landscape. A survey made in the city of Santander indicated that 30 streets are named after the names and battles won by Francoists and 12 monuments exalt the feats of the winners. In Melilla, the Spanish city of northern Africa, the Ministry of Defense refuses to withdraw two plaques commemorating the coup d'état and victory of Franco's troops. This information was published by *El País,* on February 18 and 19, 2001 by Delgado and Cué, respectively, under the titles, "El franquismo sigue en el callejero" and "Defensa se niega a retirar simbolos franquistas de Melilla," pp. 27 and 20.

The two democratic powers France and Great Britain, along with the Soviet Union, remained cautious and held on to their foreign policy forged on the crisis of the mid-1930s. The first two kept a low profile and continued their "policy of appeasement" with regard to Hitler and Mussolini's strategies, to avoid a total war similar to the Great War. The Soviet government also reacted in accordance with its search for France and Britain's support to prevent German expansionism, even if later it did provide support for the Republic. By August 1936, all European governments approved a nonintervention plan, whose effect, according to Moradiellos (2000), proved lethal to the war effort of the Republic and favorable to Franco's band. In fact, the nonintervention plan did not affect Franco's side because he received support throughout the war years and well into the 1940s from the Axis powers.

The insurrection gave rise to almost three years of civil war and forced the last government assembly to take place on February 1, 1939, in the city of Figueras, close to the French border. Five days later, the president of the Republic, Manuel Azaña, and the two presidents of the autonomous regions, Companys of Catalonia and Aguirre of the Basque country, along with ministers and members of parliament, crossed the border into France, effectively putting an end to the Republic on February 6, 1939. In the coming weeks, about a half million people would flee the country to become refugees in France. Many died in concentration camps, others sought asylum in different countries, and a number of them went back to Spain (J. L. Abellán, 1976; Bermejo, 1996; Borrás i Dolera, 2000; Caudet, 1997; Duran, 2000).

When all was over and Franco was proclaimed the head of state, he refused to declare an amnesty for the vanquished. Instead, concentration camps, jails, and summary executions took place regularly until 1969, when legislation made obsolete the transgressions committed before April 1, 1939 (Juliá, 1999). Thus, for the duration of the regime, an internal reflection on the Civil War was made impossible. Monuments, parades, text books, and documentaries all legitimized and exalted the victors. The crusade had triumphed, and the losers could only oppose through their silence. Those who remained abroad felt encouraged to reconstitute a government in exile when the military regime was condemned at the Yalta and Potsdam meetings and the United Nations rebuffed Spain. In 1946, 10 countries in Europe and Latin America recognized the Republic in exile, and this isolation of Franco's government re-ignited hope on the swift restoration of democracy (Alted, 1993). That would only take place, however, after the dictator's death. In June 1977, the first democratic elections in 40 years initiated the process of a political transition in Spain and ended the Republicans' claim. The government in exile accepted both the results of the election and the constitutional monarchy headed by King Juan Carlos I, who had been nominated by Franco in July 1969 as his successor. Yet the democratic government refused in 1986 to commemorate the 50th anniversary of the Civil War, and both the Spanish

Guardia Civil and the army continue, to this day, to jealously guard its secret archives.[7]

After all these years of painstaking silence and self-imposed taboos, Tom Clancy's irreverent novel appeared out of the blue. With its striking statements and postmodern clichés, it reminded Spaniards of a Basque question not resolved, an unfading Catalan nationalism, and a fascism that is rearing its head under a renewed impulse from the neo-Nazi movements pervading the rest of Europe (see Casals i Meseguer, 1998). In the face of this challenge, Chomsky's celebrated phrase, expressed under different conditions, reflects the situation very well: "What is that history, that is so ugly, that it must be concealed by fables?" (as cited in Peck, 1987, p. 8).

CRITICAL GEOPOLITICS AND CHOMSKY'S THEORY OF BIASED INFORMATION

In their influential book, *Manufacturing Consent,* Herman and Chomsky (1988) stated that there are forces that ensure the mass media will play the role of propagandists and transmit biased information. The media's choices, emphases, and omissions can often be understood best by analyzing them in such terms. Chomsky's propaganda model described the forces that cause the mass media to play a propaganda role, the processes whereby they mobilize bias, and the patterns of news choices that ensue. He and coauthor Herman disclosed the techniques by which the media implement the propaganda assumptions of state policy. They argued that the "naturalness" of these processes, with inconvenient facts allowed sparingly and within the proper framework of assumptions, and with dissent virtually excluded, makes for a propaganda system that is far more credible and effective in putting over a patriotic agenda than one with official censorship. Thus the media provide some facts about an issue, and literally suppress many more. Even more important, however, is the level of attention given to a fact: its placement, tone, and repetitions; the framework of analysis within which it is presented; and the related facts that accompany it and give it meaning (or preclude understanding).

One of the central themes developed by Chomsky (Herman & Chomsky, 1988) is that the observable patterns of campaigns and suppressions, of shading and emphasis on issues, and of selection of context, premises, and general agenda are

---

[7] As recently as 1991, the Official Journal of the Guardia Civil would publish laudatory articles on its participation in Nazi attacks during World War II, as reported by Cesar Ibañez Cagna in "La Division Azul y la Guardia Civil" published in *Guardia Civil. Revista Oficial y Profesional*, on October 1991, number 570, pp. 80–86. The "Division Azul" consisted of a contingent of about 60,000 Spanish personnel who fought alongside the Axis powers until 1943, although the Division still kept personnel in Riga, Berlin, and Paris until it was totally dismantled on February 14, 1944.

highly responsive to the needs of governments and major power groups. Chomsky's observation outlined the subject matter of critical geopolitics. This subdiscipline is concerned as much with maps of states and the practice of statecraft as with maps of meaning, and refers to a plural ensemble of representational practices diffused throughout societies by dailies, magazines, novels, or movies (Agnew, 1998; Dalby, 1991; Dodds, 2000; O'Tuathail & Dalby, 1998). Its methodology is based on the poststructural movement of thinkers such as Derrida, Foucault, and Bourdieu, who followed different routes to unsettle truth claims in the human sciences and challenged positivist approaches while proposing analytical alternatives. Poststructural approaches focus on the historical construction and imposition of particular discourses. One of the objectives of critical geopolitics concerns the analysis of practices that involve the development of a "script" and storytelling, such as the media's account of world events, or works of fiction such as Clancy's novel. In them a collection of attributes, scenarios, and descriptions that define places within the context of foreign policy may be identified. Besides, critical geopolitics aids the investigation of how descriptions of places and people are stitched together to narrate and explain events. Critical geopolitics diverges from geopolitics of the traditional kind. Instead of identifying the influence of geographical factors (the oceans, the land mass, the earth's riches) on the formation of foreign policy, it tends to explore how policy makers construct their representations of the world—and, most important, how their standpoints affect the interpretations of places and groups of persons (Dalby, 1991; Folch-Serra, 2000).

THE THRILLER

Tom Clancy wrote *Balance of Power* employing all the available classical postmodern techniques—and I do not mean *classical* as an oxymoron. By now, the combination of fact and fiction has become so established that few contemporary writers remain solely confined to imagined worlds to build up their works. Fact and fiction mix freely, with so-called factoids pervading all kinds of fiction. In this thriller, real-life people commingle with imagined characters. King Juan Carlos, Crown Prince Felipe, and Prime Minister Aznar share their fates with the United States' President Michael Lawrence and Colonel Brett Van Buren August, commander of the fictional Op-Center's deployment force. This liberal use of postmodern pastiche has incensed the Spanish publishers.

It is not just the characters, but historical and contemporary geopolitics that are freely mixed with the fixtures of Clancy's imagined world. He mentions "a civil war that pitted the aristocracy, the military, and the Roman Catholic Church against insurgent Communists and other anarchic forces" (p. 7) but does not remind the reader of the democratic government that was toppled by a military coup. He then adds an actual right-wing coup attempt that took place in 1981, and whose protagonists, real-life Spanish military—Armada, Milans del Bosch, and

Tejero—attempted to bring Franco's system back into the Spanish polity. Besides, to enhance the reader's interest, some of the characters discuss real contemporary politics, from the breakup of the Soviet Union and Yugoslavia to the secessionist movement in Quebec and the rising ethnocentrism in the United States.

This is a clever device. It brings about a lively story, and the reader's imagination is constantly captivated through real political references. For example, President Ferdinand Marcos's real battle with Moro secessionists exists in tandem with the capture and torture of loyal U.S. undercover agents by fictional Kurdish extremists who attempt to start a war between Turkey and Syria. Clancy also plays with time and place to portray an unstable world. One of the characters remembers his Catalonian ancestors raising sheep in the fields of León (well removed from present Catalonia!). One does not make sense of this geographical distortion, but this is precisely the point. Clancy's novel does not pretend to correctly document history and geography. Quite clearly, it is meant to be an amusing piece without pretense of veracity. As the translators have noticed, however, there is an underlying ideology permeating Clancy's fiction.

Clearly, minority nationalism and ethnicity are construed as enemies of democracy and social order, whether expressed by Kurds, Moros, Basques, Catalans, Castilians, or Quebequers. In the novel, it is asserted that "Catalonians ... were a key force in spurring on the Spanish civil war sixty years ago" (p. 89) and "are male supremacists who hate black Africans" (p. 90), while the Basques fare not much better. Thus, for Clancy, the Spanish civil war becomes a simplistic device to uphold a plot and produce a novel of suspense. Perhaps no one should demand historical accuracy from a piece made to entertain. And yet, alongside these fictional opinions, Clancy keeps introducing real historical events such as the truckloads of Nazi booty sent from Switzerland to Portugal during World War II by Franco's government, and the commissioning of drug smugglers by the Spanish defense minister in the 1980s to kill Basque separatists.[8]

I could go on showing the clever mixture of fact and fiction in Clancy's work, but the point is that an underlying political discourse can be discerned in his fiction. As Chomsky demonstrated, sometimes the media (and fiction as well) leave out specific things, but even more insidiously (because it affects the way we see everything), they leave out entire concepts, without which our world makes no sense. Or, the omission can even create a false sense of meaning, enhancing the unique way in which mythic thought operates. This applies both to Clancy's work and to the Spanish translation. The selection of facts and concepts is not a random decision; it is intentional, and the motivation for so doing may be discerned through a close reading of the text. For example, the translators omit the notion of ethnicity brought up by Clancy in the original. According to Spanish

---

[8] The case of the "GALS" (the hired thugs) had such an impact on Spanish politics that it brought to an end the 15 years of socialist government.

mythology, prevalent in Franco's brand of national Catholicism, Spain is made up of a single people.[9]

THE SPANISH TRANSLATION

In the preface of the Spanish translation, Clancy's Spanish publishers expressed a view that the author's choice of Spain as the thriller's location is due to the prestige of its NATO and EU membership, but, more important, because it is a stable country. They solemnly declare that "folkloric" Spain is now gone for good, and remark that today it is an example of harmony. Even so, one must be vigilant, they insist, otherwise Spain could become once again a site for terrorism. Following their own advice, the editors themselves become "vigilant" in this work of fiction. They think it appropriate to censor and change the text to correct an "incorrect" portrayal of Spanish reality. The novel's sense of irony eludes them. By altering the text to introduce a measure of "reality" into it and make it more "Spanish," so to speak, they accomplish a mission. For example, they mention the Cesid—the Spanish intelligence agency—alongside Interpol and the fictitious U.S. armed force, the Op-Center, as the agencies that will end the conspiracy against the Spanish state. Although Clancy does not mention the Cesid as such. Nonetheless, the publishers' patriotism and sense of national pride cannot allow for this absence.

To justify the text's changes, the publishers label as "exaggerations" the purely fictional situations of the narrative, and concur with the "understandable" indignation that the novel has raised in Spain because of these exaggerations. However, from where does this indignation come? Who has expressed it? These are puzzling questions, and the readers are not informed from where it comes. Nonetheless, the publishers take on themselves the task of correcting distortions and errors. Hence, they furnish the thriller with what they believe to be a realistic image of Spain so that no Spanish citizen or foreign visitor will ever believe the false image that Clancy has portrayed in the novel. They substitute the Royal Palace for a mansion on the outskirts of Madrid. They change the last names of some of the main characters, avoid the word *ethnic* and the concept of ethnicity, and turn the limousines into regular automobiles "because politicians in Spain do not travel in limousines" (p. 6). All these alterations are justified by the publisher's lofty wish to protect and not falsify the sociopolitical reality of Spain.

So far, these are only the preface's explanations. Deep into the translation, the bad guys are given, nonetheless, names according to their ethnic origin. Thus a Catalan must have a Catalan name (Puig) instead of a Castilian name (Ramírez, which was the name Clancy had given to his character). In Clancy's original fic-

---

[9] Franco's slogan for Spain was *Unidad de destino en lo universal*, which roughly means "Spain is a single unit, with a single destiny within the universal order of things."

tion, war puppets ask the Catalans if they are willing to consider "genocide" against other ethnic groups. The translation substitutes *armed conflict* for this more visceral term. Having set the tone for the changes, the publishers enable the reader to now go ahead and not be shocked by the fictionality of fiction. However, do the publishers really think that by their censoring and altering a work of fiction the readers will not be tricked into substituting fact for fiction? Their eagerness to counter the possibility of the novel's swaying public opinion is such that they resort to other strategies as well. Noted by a reviewer of the literary supplement of the Spanish daily *El País*[10] is the fact that two of the original novel's female agents face sexual predators in a Madrid street. In the novel these women know that if they call the police, the officers will simply join in the harassment. This is another of the "errors" that the translation "remedies." In the Spanish version, these American women suffer only the slight inconvenience of flirtatious remarks, and throughout the book they encounter sanitized Spanish police.

According to the thriller, a struggle is going on between the poor Andalusians and the rich and influential Castilians. The translation, however, reflects only minor tensions between farmers and the central government. This version, furthermore, does away with the novel's bloody ethnic conflict that Clancy had depicted as a contagious war capable of spreading to other European countries. The conflict is originated by a group of rich Catalans, whose powerful headman decides to govern Spain. The bankers of the group orchestrate a national economic catastrophe while taking advantage of the restless Basques. In Clancy's original novel, the Spanish government bribes journalists to prevent them from reporting this debacle. In the translation, the journalists are silent because their government appeals to their patriotism. According to Clancy, the real danger to the stability of the Spanish state comes from the Castilians who dream of returning Spain to its true people after a thousand years of oppression from Madrid. Considering themselves pure-blooded Spaniards, they congregate around General Amadori, who is supported by many politicians, businesspeople, and military men. In the translation, however, this general is a lunatic who has contacts with European far-right organizations and who lives with his soldiers in an abandoned 19th-century mansion.

CENSORSHIP AND CONTROL

A tradition of information control dating back to authoritarian times precedes the publishers' alterations. It began during the Civil War with a complex system of instructions, watchwords, and censorship and continued after the military insurrection's triumph in 1939. The Spanish population was exhorted to "obey, avoid

---

[10]The critique of Justo Navarro appeared on the February 27, 1999 issue of *Babelia*, p. 3 under the title, "La apuesta patriotica del traductor." *El País*, February 27, 1999.

gossip and practice an enthusiastic silence" by the periodical *Destino* (Sinova, 1989, p. 31). This kind of admonition also excused censorship and equated it to a national institution. The censors, fond of defending their trade, saw the watchword sent to all dailies "as a light in the horizon, a sign of security and a guide" (Sinova, 1989, pp. 32–33). Censorship went beyond watchwords and red pencil. In the *fiesta del libro* celebrated in Madrid on May 2, 1939, a mountain of books was publicly set on fire to erase "the ideological traces that could refer to the Spain of the losers." In the daily *Arriba* the conflagration was said to contribute to Spain's edification by condemning to the fire separatist, liberal, Marxist, anti-Catholic, romantic, pessimist, modernist, shabby, and pseudoscientific books (Sinova, 1989, p. 35).

News that compromised the regime's geopolitical objectives was not published. Such was the case, for example, with Russian advances on the Polish border against Nazi Germany on January 6, 1944. Censorship reflected the regime's brand of geopolitics through a press that was a mirror of the Second World War's evolution. At the beginning, the dailies had strict watchwords to appear neutral, then they surrendered to Berlin's instructions, and finally they argued that Spain had excellent relations with the winners of the war (Sinova, 1989, p. 221). Then, in 1968, Las Cortes (the Constituent Assembly) approved the Law of Official Secrets, which allowed the state to declare classified all those issues that it judged had to remain secret (Barrera 1995, p. 77). The media, for example, did not report Guinea's independence from Spain (ibid.). Censorship encompassed all walks of life, from moral customs to sports to publicity. Even publications like the Vatican's *L'Osservatore Romano* were prohibited for extended periods (Barrera, 1995, p. 269).

An initial step toward freedom of information began when the new Press and Printing Law of 1966 took effect (Folch-Serra & Nogué-Font, 2001). This law, according to Terron Montero, represented a compromise between the freedom of the press in democratic countries and the system of control imposed in Spain since 1938 (Terron Montero, 1981, p. 188). But even if preliminary censorship was downplayed, a system of economic sanctions was put in place that lasted until March 29, 1977 (Terron Montero, 1981, pp. 220–254).[11] The ambiguity of the law made it look liberal in some of its principles, but in fact it continued to exert control over the press and bestowed full power to the Ministry of Information to determine what could or could not be published (Barrera, 1995, pp. 96–97). What the law did, in fact, was to suppress the 30-year-old enforced censorship and imposition of watchwords. In its place came the voluntary consultation to the Ministry, which gave way to self-censorship. Sanctions for printing disallowed material could entail the destitution of the publication's manager, and heavy economic fines. In this order of things,

---

[11] It was during the mandate of Manuel Fraga Iribarne as Minister of Information and Tourism, that the Press and Printing Law of March 18, 1966, was promulgated (Chuliá, E. 2001 *El poder y la palabra*. Madrid: Editorial Biblioteca Nueva, p. 149; *The Press in Catalonia in the Eighties* (1988) Barcelona: Generalitat de Catalunya, p. 28).

most of the population was systematically uninformed and weary of change. The status quo was equated with order and peace (López Pintor, 1982, p. 80). On Franco's death in 1975, freedom of information remained imperceptible for a long while. Censorship is now a thing of the past, but a particular kind of self-restraint endures in the Spanish media. Idiosyncratic forms of censorship such as the translation of Clancy's book might indicate that some institutions of the body politic, after a long period of repression, remain conditioned by habits of the past.

CONCLUSIONS

There are several points to be made by way of conclusion. First, minority nationalism, ethnic identity, and geopolitics are a best-seller's winning combination at this particular time. If the role of the United States as policeman of the world is added to the mix, the narrative becomes even more potent. Second, as Chomsky amply demonstrated, popular literature and the media do have an influence on public opinion (Herman & Chomsky, 1988). Third, the Spanish translators of Clancy's work are very much aware of the power of the written word and have taken all possible measures to counteract an image of Spain that they perceive as deleterious.

However, their corrections underscore a lack of confidence in the strength of the state, and reveal a fear of its fragility. Clancy's best-seller touched on several key points of the Spanish polity. One of them is the country's anti-Catalan sentiment, amply documented in recent books and debates (see Bru de Sala & Tusell, 1998; Juliá, 1999; Palou, 1999). Catalan nationalism alarms many of Spain's public figures. For example, statements such as the following highlight some of the fears apparent in the Spanish translation of Clancy's book:

> In Spain it looks as though minority nationalism (*nacionalismos periféricos*) would insist on awakening a Hispanic nationalism that, after having been first identified and then sunken alongside Francoism, everyone believed that it was gone for good. It is frightening to think of the mere possibility of its renaissance. The clash of a revived Spanish nationalism and peripheral nationalism would have such terrible consequences for a peaceful assembly of all Spaniards, that the single thought of such an event leaves everything in the air, from the unity of the state to the democratic system of government. (Palou, 1999, p. 24, my translation)

The other burning point is the threat of Basque separatism always looming on the horizon. All in all, the idiosyncrasies of the Spanish translation reveal that the publishing establishment takes the media's influence on public opinion very seriously. And this apprehension also helps the publishers to freely justify in the preface their application of residual censorship practices entrenched throughout 40 years of dictatorship. Finally, even the book cover of the translation reflects and enforces both the idea of national unity and the denial of ethnic political divisions within Spain—as opposed to the bloody, contagious war in NATO's south flank

Figure 1. Two different book covers. The Spanish edition shows the pediment of the Palace of Congress and the Spanish flag. Clancy's original soft-cover denotes a neutral environment emphasizing computer technology.

imagined by Clancy (see Figure 1). Above the author's name, a statement declares that this is a polemical novel set in Spain. However, the readers need not worry about the integrity of the nation-state: A flowing Spanish flag on top of the solid, classical pediment of the Palace of Congress is presented as a symbol of endurance implying that no work of fiction can ever shake up the myth of national unity. The quest for a 'true' signification and the dismissal of ethnic divisions and cultural differences is thus visually reinforced from the very outset by this transcendental and humorless approach. Frankly, though, the readers' intelligence is put into doubt. Surely many of them could have laughed at, and enjoyed most, the thriller's incongruous statements, had they been left as they were in the original.

ACKNOWLEDGMENTS

A grant by the European Science Foundation of the European Union, allowed me to present this paper at the 1999 International Conference on Territory, Identity, and Politics in Obernai, France. I thank Simon Dalby and Don Cartwright for helpful suggestions on earlier drafts.

REFERENCES

Abellán, J. L. (Ed.). (1976). *El exilo Español de 1939* (The Spanish Exile of 1939). Madrid, Spain: Taurus.
Abellán, J. L. (1983). *De la guerra civil al exilio republicamo* (From civil war to republican exile). Madrid, Spain: Mezquita.
Abellán, J. L. (1990). *La otra cara del exilio: La diaspora del 39* (The Exile's other side: The 1939 Spanish diaspora). Madrid, Spain: Universidad Complutense.
Abellán, M. L. (1980). *Censura y creación literarias en España (1939–1976)* (Censorship and literature in Spain, 1939–1976). Barcelona, Spain: Península.
Agnew, J. (1998). *Geopolitics*. London: Routledge.
Alted, A. (1993). *El archivo de la Republica Española en el exilio, 1945–1977 (Inventario del fondo de Paris)* (The archive of the Spanish Repulic in exile, 1945–1977 [Inventory of the Paris holdings]). Madrid, Spain: Fundación Universitaria Española.
Alted, A. (Ed.). (1996). *Entre el pasado y el presente: Historia y memoria* (Between the past and the present: History and memory). Madrid, Spain: UNED.
Barrera, C. (1995). *Periodismo y franquismo* (Journalism and Francoism in Spain). Barcelona, Spain: Ediciones Internacionales Universitarias.
Bermejo, B. (Ed.). (1996). *Emigración y exilio españoles en Francia ,1936–1946* (Spanish migration and exile in France, 1936–1946). Madrid, Spain: Euderna.
Borràs i Dolera, M. (2000). *Refugiats/des (1936–39)* (Spanish refugees from 1936 to 1939). Gerona, Spain: Cuaderns de la Revista de Girona, No. 87.
Boyarin, J. (Ed.). (1994). *Remapping memory: The politics of timespace*. Minneapolis: University of Minnesota Press.
Bradley, K. (1999, March 25). Spain's history makes it odd choice to go after Pinochet. *The National Post*, p. 9.
Bru de Sala, X., & Tusell, J. (Eds.). (1998). *España Catalunya: Un diálogo con futuro* (Spain/Catalonia: A dialogue with hope). Barcelona, Spain: Planeta.
Candau, J. (1998). *Mémoire et identité* (Memory and identity). Paris: Presses Universitaires de France.
Casals i Meseguer, X. (1998). *La tentación neofascista en España* (The neo-fascist temptation in Spain). Barcelona, Spain: Plaza Janés.
Caudet, F. (1997). *Hipótesis sobre el exilio republicano de 1939* (A hypothesis on the 1939 Spanish Republican Exile). Madrid, Spain: Fundación Universitaria Española.
Chuliá, E. (2001). *El poder y la palabra* (The word and the power). Madrid, Spain: Editorial Biblioteca Nueva.
Clancy, T., & Pieczenik, S. (1998). *Op-Center: Balance of power*. New York: Berkley.
Clancy, T. (1999). *Op-Center: Equilibrio de poder*. Barcelona, Spain: Planeta.
Connerton, P. (1989). *How societies remember*. Cambridge, England: Cambridge University Press.
Cué, C. (2001, February 19). Defensa se niega a retirar símbolos franquistas de Melilla (The ministry of defense refuses to withdraw Francoist symbols from Melilla city). *El Pais*, p. 20.
Dalby, S. (1991). Critical geopolitics: Discourse, difference, and dissent. *Environment and Planning D: Society and Space, 9*, 261–283.
Delgado, J. (2001, February 18) El franquismo sigue en el callejero (Francoism continues in streetnames and monuments). *El País*, p. 27.
Dodds, K. (1998). Enframing Bosnia. In G. O'Tuathail & S. Dalby (Eds.), *Rethinking geopolitics* (pp. 170–197). London: Routledge.
Dodds, K. (2000). *Geopolitics in a changing world*. Harlow, England: Prentice Hall.
Duran, L. (Ed.). (2000). *Homenatge al President Lluis Companys* (Homage to President Lluis Companys of Catalonia). Barcelona, Spain: Generalitat de Catalunya, Departament de la Presidencia.

Folch-Serra, M. (2000). Geopolitics, globalization and self-determination (Geopolitica, globalitzacio y auto-determinacio). *Transversal, 13*, 44–49.
Folch-Serra, M., & Nogué-Font, J. (2000). Del local al global: Societat civil, premsa i territori a Catalunya (From local to global: Civil society, press and territory in Catalonia). *Revista de Catalunya, Nova etapa: Març, 149*, 9–35.
Folch-Serra, M., & Nogué-Font, J. (2001). Civil society, media and globalization in Catalonia. In M. Keating and J. McGarry (Eds.), *Minority nationalism and the changing international order*. Oxford, England: Oxford University Press, 155–178.
García Jiménez, J. (1980). *Radiotelevisión y politica cultural en el franquismo* (Cultural politics during Francoism: Radio and television). Madrid, Spain: CSIC, Instituto "Balmes" de Sociología.
Gillis, J. R. (Ed.). (1994). *Commemorations: The politics of national identity*. Princeton, NJ: Princeton University Press.
Guibernau, M. (2000). Nationalism and intellectuals in nations without states: The Catalan case. *Political Studies, 48*, 989–1005.
Halbwachs, M. (1950). *La mémoire collective (The collective memory)*. Paris: PUF.
Halbwachs, M. (1994). *Les cadres sociaux de la mémoire* (The social frames of memory). Paris: Albin Michel. (Original work published 1925)
Haro Tecglen, E. (2001, May 24). Visto/Oido: No Condenar (Seen and not heard: Do no condemn). *El País*, p. 53.
Herman, E. S., & Chomsky, N. (1988). *Manufacturing consent: The political economy of the mass media*. New York: Pantheon.
Hobsbawm, E., & Ranger, T. (1983). *The invention of tradition*. Cambridge, England: Cambridge University Press.
Hooper, J. (1995). *The new Spaniards*. Harmondsworth, England: Penguin.
Ibañez Cagna, C. (1991, October) La division azul y la guardia civil (The Blue Division and the Civil Guard). *Guardia civil. Revista oficial y profesional, 570*, 80–86.
Juliá, S. (Ed.). (1999). *Víctimas de la guerra civil* (Victims of the Spanish Civil War). Madrid, Spain: Temas de Hoy, Colección Historia.
Juliá, S. (2001, January 28). Sombras del pasado (Shadows of the past). *El País*, p. 27.
Le Goff, J. (1988). *Histoire et memoire* (History and memory). Paris: Gallimard.
Llobera, J. (1996). *The role of historical memory in (Ethno)nation-building*. London: Goldsmith's College.
López Pintor, R. (1982). *La opinión pública española: Del franquismo a la democracia* (From Francoism to democracy: A survey of Spanish public opinion). Madrid, Spain: Centro de Investigaciones Sociológicas.
Loraux, N. (1997). *La cité divisée. L'oubli dans la mémoire d'Athenes* (A divided city: Oblivion and memory in Athens). Paris: Editions Payot & Rivages.
Madalena, J. I. (1996). La memoria y el poder: Los cambios en la denominacion de las calles de Valladolid, Salamanca y Léon (Memory and power: Street name-change in Valladolid, Salamanca and León). In A. Alted (Ed.), *Entre el pasado y el presente: Historia y memoria* (pp. 143–162). Madrid, Spain: UNED.
Moradiellos, E. (2000). *La España de Franco (1939–1975): Política y sociedad* (Franco's Spain, 1939–1975: Politics and society). Madrid, Spain: Editorial Síntesis.
Nora, P. (1984). De la République à la nation (From republic to nation). In P. Nora (Ed.), *Les lieux de mémoire* (Realms of memory, Vol. 1, pp. i–xxxii). Paris: Gallimard.
Orwell, G. (1952). *Homage to Catalonia*. New York: Harcourt.
Orwell, G. (1985/1970) *Homenaje a Cataluña*, translation by Carlos Pujol. Barcelona, Spain: Editorial Seix Barral.
O'Tuathail, G., & Dalby, S. (1998). *Rethinking geopolitics*. London: Routledge.
Palou, J. (1999). El País, La Quinta Columna: L'anticatalanisme d'esquerres (*El País*, The fifth column: Anticatalanism of the left). Palma, Spain: Ediciones Documenta Balear.
Peck, R. (Ed.). (1987). *The Chomsky reader*. New York: Pantheon.

Plenn, A. (1946). *Wind in the olive trees: Spain from the inside*. New York: Book Find Club.
Preston, P. (1993). *Franco. A biography*. London: HarperCollins.
Preston, P. (1995). *The politics of revenge. Fascism and the military in 20th century Spain*. London: Routledge.
Preston, P. (1999). *"¡Comrades! Portraits from the Spanish Civil War*. London: Fontana.
Sharp, P. J. (1998). Reel geographies of the new world order. In G. O'Tuathail & S. Dalby (Eds.), *Rethinking geopolitics* (pp. 152–169). London: Routledge.
Sinova, J. (1989). *La censura de prensa durante el franquismo (1936–1951)* (Press censorship during Francoism, 1936–1951). Madrid, Spain: Espasa Calpe.
Terron Montero, J. (1981). *La prensa en España durante el régimen de Franco* (The press in Spain during Franco's regime). Madrid, Spain: Centro de Investigaciones Sociológicas.
Thomas, H. (1986). *The Spanish Civil War*. London: Hamilton.
Todorov, T. (1995). *Les abus de la mémoire* (The misuse of memory). Paris: Arla.
Veyne, P. (1978). *Comment on écrit l'histoire suivi de Foucault révolutionne l'histoire* (How do we write history after Foucault's revolution). Paris: Seuil.
Vilar, P. (1986). *La guerra civil española* (The Spanish Civil War). Barcelona, Spain: Grijalbo Mondadori.

Book Review

Charmaine L. Wijeyesinghe and Bailey W. Jackson, III (Eds.). *New Perspectives on Racial Identity Development: A Theoretical and Practical Anthology.* New York: New York University Press, 2001, 281 pp., ISBN 0-8147-9342-8 (hard), 0-8147-9343-6 (soft).

Reviewed by Jean Phinney
Department of Psychology
California State University

The study of identity development in mainstream psychology has focused on the individual and the process by which he or she forges an identity, typically during adolescence and young adulthood. This process includes a consideration of past experiences and identifications, present abilities and interests, and options for the future, leading to decisions that form the basis of one's ego identity. Erikson stressed also the role of the community and the broader context in which the adolescent resides, which define the range of options from which the adolescent can make choices. However, until recently there has been little recognition of the importance of group membership as an aspect of identity formation. Group identity in mainstream psychology has been studied primarily by social psychologists—a notable example is the Social Identity Theory of Tajfel and colleagues. Research in this tradition has examined the characteristics and implications of group identity primarily among adults, with little attention to how such identity develops.

Independent of these two dominant approaches is a parallel approach to identity that has been pursued largely by ethnic minority scholars, primarily African Americans, dealing with racial identity. There has been little connection between the work on racial identity and either the ego identity or social identity literatures. Nevertheless, the various models of racial identity have played an important role in providing a way of understanding the experiences of racial minority groups in the United States. These models and this area of research have been discussed in scattered articles and chapters, but there has not been a single source that brings together a range of scholars who have made contributions to this topic. The book under review, therefore, is a useful resource. For anyone outside this topic area, the book gives an overview of racial identity models and applications of racial identity

---

Requests for reprints should be sent to Jean Phinney, Department of Psychology, California State University, Los Angeles, CA 90032-8227.

theory. For those who know the field, it provides current summaries of familiar work, and some of the chapters go well beyond the familiar material to provide new insights and integrations.

In contrast to ethnic identity, which involves a sense of belonging to a group defined primarily by cultural or national origin, racial identity is based on the socially constructed concept of race. Racial identity development is concerned largely with responses to racism, which can be defined as assumptions or beliefs that certain racial groups, identified by their appearance, are inferior, and the resulting prejudice and discrimination against members of these groups. The early work on this topic dealt primarily with African Americans. As described in the historical survey in chapter 1, several Black identity models were proposed initially in response to the changes taking place during the Civil Rights movement in the 1960s and early 1970s, when African Americans began to reject dominant beliefs about and attitudes toward them and develop new bases of self-respect and group affirmation. These early models of Black identity have been extended in various ways, and they have spawned models of racial identity for Asian Americans, Latinos, Native Americans, biracial people, and, more recently, White Americans. Several of the chapters of the book summarize these existing models. Other chapters explore new ideas and conceptions of racial identity for particular groups or examine commonalities across groups.

The chapter by Ferdman and Gallegos, on Latinos in the United States, challenges the notion of stages of development and explores the complexities of group identity for Latinos. The chapter presents an insightful discussion of the confusion of race and ethnicity. Although this confusion exists for other ethnic groups, it is particularly salient for Latinos, who can be classified racially as White, Black, Indian, or mixed. The authors note that Latinos "both transcend and challenge the predominant categories" (p. 42). The authors emphasize the tremendous heterogeneity that characterizes Latinos and also call attention to the fluidity of group identity, changing with time and context. Rather than stages of identity formation, the authors see patterns or orientations that represent different ways of being Latino in the United States.

A more recent addition to the racial identity literature is the work on White identity development. Chapter 5, by Hardiman, describes two models of White identity development that differ somewhat but share a view of White identity development as a progression from lack of awareness of race and internalized racist attitudes, through a period of anxiety over racial issues and questioning of dominant attitudes, leading to the development of a positive White identity that is free of racism. Hardiman raises a number of important questions related to the study of White identity. For example: Is there anything more to White identity than attitudes toward other groups? Beyond issues of racism and dominance, is there some positive cultural identification possible for White Americans that is different from the multicultural blend of cultures that Americans from many backgrounds share? In this chapter, as in many of the others, virtually no data are presented either to support the models or to address these questions, and the author points out the obvious need for research.

In perhaps the most ambitious chapter, entitled "Core Processes of Racial Identity Development," Adams has as her goal to identify and describe generic processes of identity development across various racial and ethnic groups. She notes that racial identity models stem from similar historical experiences of culturally subordinated and economically marginalized ethnic communities. Each group faces parallel developmental tasks of establishing new identities not based on internalized domination or subordination. This task is accomplished through a process by which "members of devalued communities transform their consciousness of themselves and redefine their terms of negative social comparison through reaffirmations of pride and empowerment" (p. 230). This process has been discussed in the social identity literature, but there is no reference here to the earlier work. Although the models discussed in the book have in common a view of racial identity development, for minority group members, as a process of overcoming internalized racism, Adams cautions that the way this process is carried out and the cultural factors that influence it are unique to each group. In contrast to the identity task for minorities, the issue for Whites is the recognition and abandonment of entitlement or privilege.

Cross is probably the best known theorist of Black identity. In the final chapter in the book, he reviews his own and other models of racial and ethnic identity and makes a number of useful clarifications. He emphasizes that his and most other models of Black identity were developed in reference to adults—specifically, to the ways in which they become aware of and reject internalized racism—in contrast to models developed with reference to children and adolescents. Thus his model of Black identity development, which he terms *Nigrescence*, contrasts with both ego and ethnic identity development models that focus on the adolescent process of constructing an identity through increased understanding of oneself or one's ethnic group. Cross discusses both the work of Tatum, who has extended notions of racial identity downward to children, and the ethnic identity research that focuses on adolescence. Cross presents a complex but interesting model of the relationship of ego identity and Black identity formation across the life span, in one of the few attempts to bring together mainstream and racial identity models.

Two other chapters deal with applied issues—namely, the use of racial identity development in counseling situations and in mediation of conflicts—that may be of interest to individuals working in those fields.

Models of racial identity seem to capture an important dimension of the experience of racial minorities, and these models have been a focus for understanding the ethnic minority experience. They have had an important impact on areas of psychology dealing with ethnic minority issues, particularly the area of counseling, which has produced much of the writing on the topic and where the applications seem most obvious. However, these models have had relatively little impact on other areas of psychology, and it is worth speculating why that is the case. In reading this volume, one is struck by how little empirical research is reported. The basis of the models presented seems to be predominantly interview studies or clinical or counseling experience. The various models are reported descriptively, but there is little or no research where interviews have been objectively coded so that reliability can be demonstrated and specific hypotheses tested. The attempts to quantify racial identity, most notably the measure developed by Helms and Parham, are not discussed at all, perhaps because existing research has raised questions about the reliability and validity of such attempts. Thus the reader is left feeling that although racial identity models appear plausible, there may be other explanations for the phenomena of interest. The bases for racial identity theory and models have not been critically examined. The concepts presented and discussed need to be empirically tested, ideally with longitudinal studies that could trace changes over time. Several of the chapters give suggestions for research that needs to be done to advance the field. If these suggestions are followed, a clearer and more precise picture of this topic may emerge in the future. In the meantime, for those interested in understanding current thinking about racial identity, this book presents an accessible and readable overview of the topic.

Contributor Information

International and multidisciplinary in scope, this new cutting-edge journal provides a forum for identity theorists and researchers around the globe to share their ideas and findings regarding the problems and prospects of human self-definition. The unifying thread of these articles is "identity" in its various manifestations throughout the life course. The operating assumption is that people in many parts of the world are struggling with aspects of their identities, and that many of these problems transcend national, political, and cultural boundaries, taking on global proportions.

In addition to a focus on substantive theoretical and empirical analyses, the journal also welcomes policy discussions, program recommendations, and evaluation studies. The journal will provide a forum in which theoretical analyses find practical applications in dealing with these global problems. Submissions are invited from all fields and from the full range of methodologies. In these respects, the journal provides multiple bridges, across nations and disciplines, as well as between theory and research, and subjectivist and objectivist epistemologies. The intention is to provide a nonpartisan forum within which researchers from the various areas concerned with identity can communicate their findings and stay apprised of the findings of other researchers, especially among those who use different technical languages.

Readership: Personality and social psychologists; developmental/lifespan psychologists; clinical and counseling psychologists and mental health professionals in psychiatry and social work; cultural anthropologists and political scientists; historians; policy analysts concerned with social services and programs; sociologists; and those interested in cultural, educational, and gender studies.

Streamlined submission procedure: Manuscripts can now be submitted as an email attachment to cote@uwo.ca if they are in an IBM-compatible format and are in Word or WordPerfect. If the attachment cannot be downloaded, authors will be asked to send the manuscript by airmail or courier. For details: http://www.sscl.uwo.ca/sociology/identity/contributor_information.html

Manuscript Submission: Submit four manuscript copies (including four sets of illustrations, one of which is the original) to the Editor, Professor James Côté, Department of Sociology, University of Western Ontario, London, Ontario, Canada N6A 5C2 [cote@uwo.ca; tel. 519-661-2111 x85118; fax. 519-661-3200]. Prepare manuscripts according to the *Publication Manual of the American Psychological Association* (5th ed.) using U.S. English spelling. Any manuscript not in this style may be returned to the author.

The length of manuscripts should normally not exceed 30 pages, with all components double-spaced, including title page, abstract, text, quotes, acknowledgments, references, appendices, tables, figure captions, and footnotes. The abstract should be 100 to 150 words, typed on a separate sheet of paper. All copies should be clear, readable, and on $8\frac{1}{2}$ x 11-in. paper of good quality. Print text using 10-point (12-pitch) Courier or any other typeface that results in 1,800 to 2,000 characters per page (70 to 75 characters and spaces per line x 25 to 27 lines per page). Authors must use nonsexist language in their manuscripts. For information on this requirement, read "Guidelines for Nonsexist Language in APA Journals" which appeared in the June 1977 issue of the *American Psychologist* or consult the *Manual*.

All manuscripts submitted will be acknowledged promptly if an e-mail address is provided. Authors should keep a copy of the manuscript to guard against loss. All manuscripts are reviewed by scholars with special competence in the area represented by the manuscript. To facilitate the proper matching of reviewers, provide six key words. If you feel that your manuscript needs special attention, provide the names and addresses (including e-mail) of potential reviewers who can provide unbiased assessments.

Book Reviews: In addition to regular manuscripts, the editors of the journal will also accept unsolicited book reviews. Each book review should contain the author(s) name(s), title of the book, price and ISBNs for paper and cloth copies, number of pages in the book, and the publisher information and address. Two copies and a disk file of each book review should be submitted to: Book Review Editor William Kurtines, Department of Psychology, Florida International University, Miami, FL 33199. E-mail: kurtines@fiu.edu

Recommendations for Submitting Articles: It is strongly encouraged that submissions be sent by courier or some sort of express mail (like Global Priority Mail in the United States). If the submission must be sent through the regular mail system, use Air Mail. In addition, it is recommended that you e-mail the Editor to expect the package. Taking these steps will help avoid delays in providing timely reviews of manuscripts.

Permissions: Authors are responsible for all statements made in their work and for obtaining permission from copyright owners to reprint or adapt a table or figure or to reprint a quotation of 500 words or more. Authors should write to original author(s) and publisher to request nonexclusive world rights in all languages to use the material in the article and in future editions. Provide copies of all permissions and credit lines obtained.

Regulations: Only original manuscripts, written in English, are considered. In a cover letter, authors should state that the findings reported in the manuscript have not been published previously and that the manuscript is not being simultaneously submitted elsewhere. Authors should also state that they have complied with American Psychological Association ethical standards in the treatment of their samples. Upon acceptance, the authors are required to sign a publication agreement transferring the copyright from the author to the publisher. Accepted manuscripts become the permanent property of the journal.

Production Notes: After a manuscript is accepted for publication, its author must provide a computer disk containing the manuscript file. This file should be formatted for IBM computers (in WordPerfect or Word) and be clean of all irrelevant codes. Files are copyedited and typeset into page proofs. Authors read proofs to correct errors and answer editors' queries.